JINNAH

THE FOUNDER OF PAKISTAN

in the eyes of his contemporaries and his
documentary records at Lincoln's Inn
and the Inner Temple

SECOND EDITION

Compiled and edited by
Saleem Qureshi

OXFORD
UNIVERSITY PRESS

OXFORD
UNIVERSITY PRESS

No. 38, Sector 15, Korangi Industrial Area, PO Box 8214,
Karachi-74900, Pakistan

Oxford University Press is a department of the University of Oxford.
It furthers the University's objective of excellence in research, scholarship,
and education by publishing worldwide in

Oxford New York

Auckland Cape Town Dar es Salaam Hong Kong Karachi
Kuala Lumpur Madrid Melbourne Mexico City Nairobi
New Delhi Shanghai Taipei Toronto

With offices in

Argentina Austria Brazil Chile Czech Republic France Greece
Guatemala Hungary Italy Japan Poland Portugal Singapore
South Korea Switzerland Turkey Ukraine Vietnam

Oxford is a registered trademark of Oxford University Press
in the UK and in certain other countries

Published in Pakistan by Oxford University Press, Karachi

ISBN 978-0-19-906173-0

Typeset in Adobe Garamond Pro
Printed in Pakistan by
Kagzi Printers, Karachi.
Published by
Ameena Saiyid, Oxford University Press
No. 38, Sector 15, Korangi Industrial Area, PO Box 8214,
Karachi-74900, Pakistan.

CONTENTS

ILLUSTRATIONS

Lord Weatherill, The Speaker, House of Commons, 1983–1992

FOREWORD

Lives of great men all remind us,
We can make our lives sublime,
And, departing, leave behind us,
Footprints on the sands of time.

Longfellow

It is now twelve years since the inaugural meeting of the Jinnah Society was so aptly held in the Old Hall of Lincoln's Inn and I am delighted to welcome this book which records that remarkable occasion.

Quaid-i-Azam Mohammad Ali Jinnah will always be remembered as the Father of the Nation and we all today walk in his footsteps.

It was from Lincoln's Inn that he went on to become the Founder of Pakistan and I congratulate Saleem Qureshi for compiling the speeches which were delivered by his contemporaries together with the personal anecdotes of those who knew him and worked with him. In addition, Mr Qureshi has included much other interesting material and all of us who love Pakistan are greatly in his debt.

I hope the whole of the Pakistani community as well as the host community will find this book valuable, interesting, and informative.

Bernard Weatherill
1996

INTRODUCTION TO THE SECOND EDITION

My second edition includes three new chapters.

I have added a chapter on Jinnah and the Inner Temple. Not many people, even lawyers, know that Jinnah was called to the Bar by Lincoln's Inn but after practicising as a barrister in India, returned to London and was called ad eundem by the Inner Temple, practising at 11, Kings Bench Walk.

I have included selected extracts from letters by Dr Sir Mohammad Iqbal to Jinnah, as he deserves a place amongst the luminaries of Jinnah's contemporaries.

Finally, due to the recent worldwide financial crisis, I have also added a chapter on Jinnah and Islamic banking. The eminent Professor Philip Molyneux of Bangor University, UK, has contributed a section in this chapter especially for this book.

I have also expanded the section on the Retrospective view of Jinnah to include a letter to myself from Lord Irvine, The Lord Chancellor.

Saleem Qureshi
Lincoln's Inn

The editor with Elizabeth Rogers of Lincoln's Inn Archives

The editor with Celia Pilkington, Archives Officer of the Inner Temple

PREFACE

Not gold, but only men can make
A people great and strong,
Men who, for the truth and honour's sake,
Stand fast and suffer long,
Who dare, while others fly—
They build a nation's pillars deep
And lift them to the sky.

Emerson

I was present in 1965 when Mohammad Ali Jinnah's portrait was presented to the Treasurer of Lincoln's Inn by His Excellency Agha Hilali, then High Commissioner for Pakistan, in a modest ceremony held by the Inns of Court Pakistan Society. Since then, the portrait has been placed among those of other great lawyers and statesmen.

My colleagues and friends were curious to know more about this eminent lawyer-statesman who founded a new country within the comity of nations. In the past, the Inns of Court Pakistan Society, founded by Pakistani students, had held functions and provided information relating to the newly-born country and its founder; but in the late 1970s the Society disappeared as students from Pakistan ceased to come here for legal studies.

In the early 1980s, I spoke to my colleagues and senior members of the Bar about forming a society which would introduce the life and mission of Jinnah to lawyers as well as the host community. I also spoke to notable Pakistanis resident in the UK with an interest in this kind of work and received an encouraging response.

At the end of 1983, I convened a meeting in Gray's Inn with the kind permission of the late Sir Arthur Power, the Secretary of the Bar Council, (comprising members of the Bar and some non-lawyer members) with a view to forming a body called the Jinnah

Academy or Jinnah Foundation. At a subsequent meeting in my Chambers, then in Gray's Inn, Mr Justice Samdani of Pakistan supported the idea of forming a society called the M.A. Jinnah Society.

The Jinnah Society held its inaugural function in the historic Old Hall of Lincoln's Inn in April 1984. Mr Arshad was the chief guest and also present were Lord Listowel, former Secretary of State for India; Sir John Biggs-Davison; Mr Budd, QC; Ahmed E.H. Jaffer; and Lady Noon, who had all met Mr Jinnah personally. Scholars present on the occasion included Dr Gordon Johnson, Director of the Centre of South Asian Studies in Cambridge, and Professor Riazul Islam, a visiting Professor at St Anthony's College, Oxford, on a Quaid-i-Azam Fellowship.

It was a unique gathering in the Old Hall of Lincoln's Inn, with those who had known Jinnah personally contributing memoirs and anecdotes. Mr Ali Arshad, Pakistan's Ambassador to the United Kingdom strongly urged that the speeches should be published for posterity.

I therefore began to compile this publication as a collection of speeches but felt it appropriate to include other contemporary material which I hope the reader will find of interest.

Lincoln's Inn   Saleem Qureshi
May 1997

ACKNOWLEDGEMENTS

I would like to thank my friends and colleagues, especially the staff at Lincoln's Inn, the Pakistan High Commission, and the Oriental and India Office Collections of the British Library.

I would also like to extend my gratitude to the speakers at the inaugural meeting of the Jinnah Society, who made this book possible.

For the second edition, my thanks to the archives staff at the Inner Temple and to Professor Philip Molyneux.

Saleem Qureshi

JINNAH
AN INTRODUCTION

1
_____

THE GREATNESS OF JINNAH
Qutubuddin Aziz

Early in the 1980s, when I was serving as Minister for Information at the Pakistan Embassy in London, Barrister Saleem Qureshi discussed with me the need for setting up a Memorial Society in London for Quaid-i-Azam Mohammad Ali Jinnah, the founder of Pakistan. Having hero-worshipped the Quaid since 1936 when my parents ushered me into his august presence at the Cecil Hotel in Simla in pre-independence India, I heartily welcomed Mr Qureshi's laudable proposal to establish such a Memorial Society and pledged him my full support and co-operation in this laudable venture. He showed immense enterprise and devotion and assembled a band of the Quaid-i-Azam's admirers who joined him in founding the Memorial Society for the Father of the Pakistani Nation. One of their first undertakings was to organize a seminar in London to pay homage to the memory of the Quaid-i-Azam and formally to announce the formation of the Society in 1984.

When I spoke to Ambassador Ali Arshad about Barrister Qureshi's plan to establish the Memorial Society for the Quaid-i-Azam and hold a seminar on his life and work, I found him very enthusiastic and he readily accepted my proposal that he should preside over the Society's inaugural function in London with Lord Listowel, who was the Secretary of State for India at the time of the 1947 partition of the subcontinent, as the keynote speaker.

Mr Qureshi had graciously billed me as one of the speakers for the memorial meeting in London on 17 April 1984, but the Pakistani community in Manchester was holding a meeting on the same day and Ambassador Ali Arshad had earlier indicated his willingness to address it, unaware of the date subsequently fixed by Mr Qureshi for the London meeting. I, therefore, decided to deputize for the Ambassador at the Manchester meeting, denying myself the honour and pleasure of being present at the inaugural meeting of the Jinnah Memorial Society in London. But in thought and spirit I was with Barrister Qureshi and his colleagues and all those ladies and gentlemen who attended this meeting in London to pay tribute to Mohammad Ali Jinnah, the maker of Pakistan. I am exceedingly pleased that through Mr Qureshi's efforts a book based on the speeches delivered at this memorable meeting is now being published.

All through the eight years of my diplomatic assignment at the Pakistan Embassy in London (1978–86), I missed no opportunity to speak in public gatherings on the greatness of Quaid-i-Azam Mohammad Ali Jinnah. I do, indeed, consider him the greatest Muslim leader of the twentieth century. In 1935, he took up the leadership of the All-India Muslim League at a time when it was virtually rudderless and Muslim India was captive to feuding factions and beset by socio-economic frustration. Assisted by Mr Liaquat Ali Khan and a team of devoted and selfless followers, the Quaid-i-Azam transformed it, within a few years, into an organization capable of conducting a mass movement all over the length and breadth of the subcontinent for the establishment of the Muslim-majority state of Pakistan. The Quaid-i-Azam had no army at his command; he and the Muslim League lacked the financial resources which are so essential for waging a countrywide political battle. Pitted against him and his party was the might of the opulent, Hindu-dominated All-India Congress which wanted to inherit the whole of the subcontinent as its sole possession. The British Raj was also not enthusiastic about any scheme that would partition the subcontinent and weaken Britain's imperial interests in the region.

When Mahatma Gandhi spoke of India, it was a name and a territory that had existed for many thousands of years. When Quaid-i-Azam Jinnah spoke of Pakistan, it was a dream-state, the concept of which was unfolded by our great poet and philosopher, Dr Mohammad Iqbal, in 1930, and the name of which was coined in 1932 by a Cambridge-based Muslim scholar, Chaudhry Rahmat Ali, in his historic monograph entitled *Now or Never* (which was published by the Pakistan National Movement from its tiny office in Cambridge in January 1933). By 23 March 1940—the day which Pakistanis celebrate every year as Pakistan Day—the Quaid-i-Azam had succeeded in making the Muslim League such a potent and countrywide political party in India that it felt strong enough to proclaim in Lahore that the establishment of independent Muslim States, comprising the Muslim-majority areas of the subcontinent in the north-west and east, would be the goal of its political endeavours and exertions. Thus was launched the Pakistan Movement under Mr Jinnah's inspiring leadership. In seven years' time, the Quaid-i-Azam made this dream a massive reality in the shape of Pakistan which on 14 August 1947—the day of its birth—was the fifth largest state in the world and the world's biggest Muslim state.

The annals of the twentieth century in Asia have no parallel to match the glory and splendour of the Quaid-i-Azam's remarkable achievement. And for thirteen tumultuous and trying months, despite the onerous weight of his septuagenarian years and the cruelty of the lung ailment that was eating up the vitals of his physical frame, he steered, as its first Governor-General and founder, the ship of the nascent State through stormy waters and demonstrated to the world the viability of his magnificent creation– Pakistan.

As I saw the flat on Russell Road in Kensington where Mr Jinnah lived as a hard-working, teenage student studying for the

Bar in 1893, the impressive Lincoln's Inn where G.F. Watt's fresco of the world's great law-givers included the Prophet of Islam and attracted the Quaid to join it for his legal education, and the Old Vic where he gave up a tempting offer to become a Shakespearean actor because his father in Karachi opposed it, my respect for the Great Leader who gave us the blessing of Pakistan and independent nationhood rose by leaps and bounds. Much to my disappointment, the Quaid's posh, three-storeyed villa in Hampstead's West Heath Road, where he lived with his loyal sister, Fatima, and his school-going daughter, Dina, during the years of his political hibernation in London in 1930–4, is no more. Miss Fatima Jinnah, a respected friend of my mother, told me in Karachi in the 1950s that it was in this Hampstead house that letters from Allama Iqbal, the Aga Khan, Mr Liaquat Ali, and a number of other loyal friends in India persuaded the Quaid to return to the subcontinent in 1934 and take up the presidentship of the Muslim League.

I know that Lincoln's Inn had a place of eminence in the Quaid-i-Azam's memories and affections. I was indeed thrilled when Sir Frederick Bennett, himself its alumnus, proposed to us in the Embassy, in his capacity as the President of the UK-based Pakistan Society in the early 1980s, that the Society's Annual Dinner should be held in the history-laced Great Hall in Lincoln's Inn. Ambassador Ali Arshad and I were ecstatic over this splendid proposal and the event was a great success. A large portrait of the Quaid-i-Azam watched hundreds of his admirers and devotees in the august Great Hall where he, during the years 1893–6, attended the ceremonial dinners which were a part of a barrister's education and training for being called to the Bar. Many great statesmen—William Pitt, Gladstone, Disraeli, Canning, and Asquith to name a few—studied law in the sanctum of Lincoln's Inn, but none except Mr Jinnah had the unique distinction of being the founder of a new state larger than the Great Britain of today. The Pakistan Society continues to hold its Annual Dinners in the Great Hall in Lincoln's Inn, giving immense pleasure to the Quaid's immortal soul.

I feel sad that four of the eminent speakers in the 1984 Quaid-i-Azam Jinnah Seminar in London have died since then:

Ambassador Ali Arshad, the Earl of Listowel, Sir John Biggs-Davison, and Mr Ahmed E.H. Jaffer. They had known the Quaid-i-Azam and were his ardent admirers. The publication of the Seminar report will do justice to their eminent contribution to the Seminar.

My 1989 book, *Pakistan and the British Media,* has these words of gratitude and commendation for Barrister Qureshi:

> I am grateful to a young London-based Pakistani barrister, Mr Saleem Qureshi, who espoused with immense energy and passion my suggestion for the establishment of a Quaid-i-Azam Mohammad Ali Jinnah Memorial Society in London in 1983. Its seminar on the life and achievement of Pakistan's founder, held under the chairmanship of Ambassador Ali Arshad in Lincoln's Inn, was a great success. The star speaker was Lord Listowel who was Secretary of State for India at the time when the Dominions of Pakistan and India were born in August 1947. His praise for the Quaid-i-Azam was copious.

May God bless the Quaid-i-Azam M.A. Jinnah Society in London and all those associated with it.

Mr Qutubuddin Aziz served as Minister for Information at the Embassy of Pakistan (now the High Commission) in London, from 1978–86. After working in London as a diplomat, he returned to Pakistan in 1986, becoming Chairman of the semi-government National Press Trust which at that time ran nine daily newspapers and five weeklies. Having retired from government service in 1988, he now lives in Karachi. He has written a number of books and he also writes for some Pakistani newspapers. [Ed.]

2

THE GREAT LEADER

Saleem Qureshi

On behalf of the Jinnah Society, I welcome you all to this meeting, held in memory of the founder of Pakistan, a former member of Lincoln's Inn, a distinguished lawyer and statesman, and an eminent politician of his time. Quaid-i-Azam was his title which means 'great leader'; Mohammad Ali Jinnah his name.

Before I speak about the Society, I would like to say a few words about the Quaid who inspired us to form the Society. Quaid-i-Azam Mohammad Ali Jinnah was born in Karachi in 1876* on the day which was chosen by the Christian clergy to celebrate the birth of Jesus Christ, that is 25 December. Perhaps because of that blessed coincidence, he followed all those teachings of Jesus which were endorsed by the Quran and the Prophet Muhammad (peace be upon him).

Jesus performed the miracle of bringing the dead to life and was called the Messiah. Mr Jinnah was a messiah in the restricted sense that he revived the spirit of nationhood among the Muslims of India and secured a homeland for them. He chose for himself the

---

* 1876 is the officially recognized year of Jinnah's birth.

pattern of life of a prophet and followed it strictly until the last minute of his life. Yet he never projected himself as a religious leader.

Now for a brief account of his life.

After completing his school education, Mr Jinnah came to London in 1892 and joined Lincoln's Inn on 5 June 1893. He passed his Bar Examinations when he was twenty-one years of age.

Even in the days when he attended the lectures conducted by the Council of Legal Education, during his free time he would go to Westminster and watch the debates in the House of Commons from the public gallery. Lincoln's Inn was his alma mater and Westminster an informal school for politics. From these two institutions he received his legal and political training.

On his return to the subcontinent, Jinnah started his legal practice in Karachi. But this was too small a place for him and he moved to Bombay. As he did not come from a rich family, he had some difficulty in the beginning but soon established himself as a prominent lawyer in Bombay.

Jinnah had imbibed the traditions of the Inn and the ethics and etiquette of the Bar and applied them strictly to his practice, even though the discipline in India did not require such strict application of those rules.

Mr Jinnah made a name for himself and earned fame and fortune as a lawyer before entering politics. He used his wealth, skill, and legal background to achieve his ultimate political goal– Pakistan.

At the beginning of his political career, he was a staunch supporter of the Indian Congress. Later, he realized that the Congress, secular in form but religious in substance, would offer no solution to the problems of the Muslims in the subcontinent. It would rather push them to the other extreme of communism. So he called the Muslims together under the banner of the Muslim League and urged them to follow the middle path which was laid down by Islam and which was preached by the prophets Abraham, Moses, Jesus, and Muhammad (peace be upon them).

Mr Jinnah not only believed in non-violence in politics but also practised it throughout his life. He did not ever provoke others to violence either. His struggle for independence was legal and constitutional. The proof of this is that unlike many other leaders in the subcontinent, he was never arrested or sent to prison.

Jinnah knew very well that the constitution, law, and democracy were the strengths as well as the weaknesses of British politicians. So he kept his battle within the framework of the constitution and ultimately won his constitutional battle and secured a homeland for the Muslims of India only a year and one month before his final departure from this world.

JINNAH
CONTEMPORARY VIEWS

3

A BRILLIANT POLITICIAN
William Francis Listowel

It is indeed a very great honour to be asked to speak at the inaugural meeting of the Quaid-i-Azam Mohammad Ali Jinnah Society and I should like to thank Mr Qureshi and the members of the managing committee for having asked me to do so. I would also like to wish the Society, this being the first opportunity I have had to do so, the utmost success in what I hope will be a very long life in carrying out the immensely worthwhile programme which has just been explained by Mr Qureshi.

I had the privilege and good fortune to meet Quaid-i-Azam Mohammad Ali Jinnah on several occasions during the time I was a minister in the British Government—first, in an official capacity when he used to come to London representing the Muslim League, in negotiations leading up to independence in 1947, and later, as a guest at his home in Karachi just after independence. After the loss of his wife, his sister Miss Fatima Jinnah had been keeping house for him and they made me feel completely at home during the short but very pleasant visit. I was delighted to find Mohammad Ali Jinnah, in the atmosphere of his home, a relaxed and genial host, very different from the stern, unbending figure usually depicted when he was acting as spokesman for the Muslim League.

But it is naturally the political persona in which the world is mainly interested. My old friend, H.V. Hodson, in his brilliant book on the transfer of power, writes as follows about the part played by Mr Jinnah. I quote: 'Of all the personalities in the great drama óf India's rebirth to independence, Mohammad Ali Jinnah was at once the most enigmatic and the most important. One can imagine any other of the principal actors (not counting Mahatma Gandhi, who makes fitful and inconclusive appearances from the wings) replaced by a substitute in the same role—a different Congress leader, a different Secretary of State [I agree: I was Secretary of State at the time and I am sure somebody could have done exactly the same job equally well, if not better], a different representative of this or that interest or community, even a different Viceroy—without thereby implying any radical change in the final denouement. But it is barely conceivable that events would have taken the same course, that the last struggle would have been a struggle of three, not two, well-balanced adversaries, and that a new nation State of Pakistan would have been created, but for the personality and leadership of one man, Mr Jinnah.'

I agree with every word of this evaluation of the unique role of Mr Jinnah in the shaping of these two new nations.

It should be remembered that the demand for Indian independence and the British will to relinquish power in India soon after the end of the Second World War, were the result of influences which had been at work long before the last decade before 1947, whereas the demand for Pakistan, and the solidarity of the Indian Muslims behind that demand, were creations of that decade alone, and supremely the creation of one man. In order to trace the main steps which led Mr Jinnah to the conclusion that Muslims in India must have their separate homeland, we have to go back a considerable distance into the past. How did it come about that the eminent Congress leader, the idol of the *Young India* nationalists in the 1920s, the protagonist of unity between Hindus and Muslims, became the single-minded leader of his own community towards a promised land of a new Islamic nation? One thing is certain, his motives were completely disinterested. No one has ever suggested the faintest taint of corruption, nor was he in the slightest degree, like so many politicians, a political weathercock, swinging with the winds of popularity, or changing his policies to suit popular acclaim. He was a lifelong idealist, as well as a man of scrupulous honour.

What one would like to know is why, in middle life, he supplanted one ideal with another, and kept to this new ideal until the very end of his days. This conversion, while it cannot be pinpointed precisely, must have taken place some time in the early 1930s after he came to London for the Round Table Conference. After the conference was over, he settled in England, travelling around for several years before deciding to make his home in India. He made a considerable reputation as a superb advocate in the Law Courts here. Mr Qureshi has already referred to the part he played in that capacity. At the same time he was still deeply concerned about Indian freedom, and Hindu-Muslim unity, and particularly about the part his community should play in obtaining these objectives, and he spoke on several occasions in this sense.

In May 1924 he used these words at a meeting of the Muslim League at Lahore: 'The advent of foreign rule and its continuance in India was previously due to the fact that the people of India, particularly the Hindus and Muslims, were not united and did not sufficiently trust each other—I am almost inclined to say that India will get Dominion and responsible government the day the Muslims and Hindus are united.' But of course the fact was that 'sufficient trust' did not exist at the time, and distrust steadily increased as the years went by. Mr Jinnah's repeated pleas to Congress for special recognition for the Muslim minority fell on deaf ears.

In 1928, an All Parties Conference was convened to draft a constitution for a United India. It was followed by a so-called Unity Conference in Lucknow. The Muslim League wanted safeguards for a Muslim community included in the new constitution, but these were ignored or rejected by the Congress majority. It was then that

Mr Jinnah gave a warning that the inevitable result of leaving minorities with a sense of insecurity would be revolution and civil war. His warning went unheeded. As he left Calcutta for his home city of Bombay, he said to an old friend, and I quote, 'This is the parting of the ways'. Several years later he described the mood of complete disillusionment after the failure of the Round Table Conference. It was a disillusionment with the leadership of his own community as well as with the pretensions of Congress. What he said was that the Muslims were led at that time 'either by flunkies of the British Government or by the camp-followers of Congress'. He had begun to feel he could neither help India nor change the Hindu mentality.

He was rescued from this despair of politics by a visit from his old friend, Liaquat Ali Khan, who had already shown his devotion to the Muslim League and was destined to become the first Prime Minister of Pakistan. He pleaded with Mr Jinnah to return to India to lead his community and the League. Mr Jinnah took two years to make up his mind, but in October 1935 he returned for good. Speaking a year after his return at a meeting in Delhi, he used these words: 'We must think of the interests of our community; the Hindus and Muslims must be organized separately and once they are organized they will understand each other better.'

Then in 1937 came the provincial elections, when Congress refused to share with him and the Muslim League any of the ministerial posts in the provincial governments. This convinced him, if he still needed convincing, that the Muslim League would never get a fair deal from a Congress-run India. In the same year, in a speech at Lucknow, which is generally regarded as his decisive challenge to Congress, he spoke specifically of the Muslim community as a 'nation', and a 'nation' that would emerge from the struggle with the majority community, who had clearly shown their hand that 'Hindustan is for the Hindu'. Mahatma Gandhi described these words as 'a declaration of war'. It did not take long for the policy of their leader to be endorsed by his followers.

In March 1940, at the League Conference in Lahore, the historic resolution was passed which has been called the Pakistan Resolution calling for the divorce of the Muslim majority provinces from the rest of India, so that they could become a separate nation.

Mr Jinnah's estrangement from the Congress and his emergence as a purely communal champion were due to his personality as well as political conviction. His pride had been wounded by the treatment he had received from Congress and Liberal leaders since the 1920s. His grievance against them was not satisfied until he had defeated their purpose twenty years later.

Mr Jinnah was a man of principle, but he was also fiercely proud. For the Muslim community, as the ideal leader of their national cause, he had three supreme qualities: the first was his single-mindedness, his sheer strength of will, what would be called in modern parlance political will. Having set his hand to the task of uniting his community behind a demand for recognition as a nation, nothing deterred him, least of all the practical difficulties of separation which he declined even to discuss, and which he always insisted would be settled, once the principle had been accepted. The second of these qualities was the fact that he was a loner, aloof from personal or family attachments, not involved in the in-fighting of parliamentary or party politics, lacking even the Muslim roots which might have labelled him a Shia or Sunni or partisan of any particular Muhammadan tradition. This enabled him to unite all Indian Muslims as the symbol of Indian Muslim nationhood. Finally, there was the consummate tactical skill of the brilliant lawyer applied to the process of political bargaining. He knew how to take advantage of every situation, however unpromising, above all how to delay commitment, leaving opponents to make their mistakes. A point once gained, he never lost. It became the starting point to the next point to be demanded. He made rings around his less skilful antagonists, whether Indian or British, and they always gave way in the end.

Mr Jinnah's determination to bring about partition was made clear from the first of the talks with the new Viceroy, Lord Mountbatten, after the latter's arrival in India in March 1947. In his very first conversation he said he had come to tell the Viceroy exactly what he was prepared to accept. He went on to claim that there was only one solution, 'a surgical operation', without which India would perish. The Cabinet Mission Plan was valueless because it ignored the necessity for the operation. He was 'absolutely adamant that it was useless to revive the Cabinet Mission Plan'. When the Viceroy replied that the argument for partition applied equally to the Punjab and Bengal, he admitted the logic of the statement, but implored Mountbatten not to give him a 'moth-eaten' Pakistan. He thought the demand for partitioning these provinces was a bluff by Congress to frighten him off his claim for Pakistan. To this the Viceroy replied: 'If I agree to partition it would be down to your able advocacy but I could not let your theories stop short at the national level.' At the next interview, Mr Jinnah insisted that Pakistan should have its own army, to which the reply was that if he decided finally upon some sort of partition, a committee of experts would be set up to divide the armed forces. And so it was.

What is remarkable about Mr Jinnah's attitude in these preliminary talks is the clarity and inflexible determination of his vision of the future: the Muslims must have their own nation-state with its own armed forces.

He would have nothing to do with the Cabinet Mission Plan or any other for providing a Constitutional Centre, because that would diminish the sovereignty of Pakistan and put him at the mercy of the untrustworthy Congress leaders. But if there were first a surgical operation, then Hindustan and Pakistan could come together to discuss and deal with matters of common concern at the national level. He rejected strongly the partition of the Punjab and Bengal, but was not to be put off by the rest of it. What he had said indicated that he was moving towards paying the price of a 'moth-eaten' Pakistan rather than no Pakistan at all. Mountbatten complained that he showed 'a complete lack of administrative knowledge'. But judgements appropriate to civil servants, as to soldiers or career politicians, cannot be applied to visionaries.

Mr Jinnah had this visionary quality. For him, politics was not, as R.A. Butler called it, 'the art of the possible', but that art of what most people thought at the time to be impossible, namely, the creation of a new country, Pakistan. His political vision was not concerned with practical difficulties, compromises, or matters of detail, but dedication to a principle which allowed no qualification, and to a purpose he was determined to achieve.

It will be remembered that Mountbatten's final plan for Indian independence was in fact for the partition of British India between India and Pakistan, with both new countries staying in the Commonwealth and obtaining their independence at the earliest possible moment. It was, of course, essential for the acceptance of their plan by the British Government that it should be agreed to by both parties, Congress and the Muslim League. This was also indispensable for its acceptance by the parliamentary Opposition at home. Without their support in the House of Commons, the Independence Bill could not have passed into law in time for the early date, 15 August 1947, envisaged for the termination of British rule. Acceptance of the plan by Congress was already assured, but the verdict of the League would depend entirely on the advice tendered by Mr Jinnah.

While admitting that the plan did not altogether meet the League point of view (of course it was allowed what he had called a 'moth-eaten' Pakistan), Jinnah declared that it was not for him but for the League's All-India Council to say whether it should be accepted as a settlement. The fact that he took the statesmanlike line of leaving the question open, by raising no objection, made it possible for the All-India League Council to endorse the plan.

What emerged from the conversations at the personal level between Mr Jinnah and Lord Mountbatten about independence was a strong, probably mutual dislike. These preliminary talks took place at critical meetings during the first fortnight of April 1947. They were the vital discussions which determined the future of the subcontinent after British rule.

Mountbatten went into them, in his own words, 'with the most enormous confidence in my ability to persuade people to do the right thing, not because I am persuasive so much as because I have the knack of being able to present things in the most favourable light'. As he would later recall, 'I tried every trick I could play, I used every appeal I could imagine, to shake Jinnah's resolve to have partition. Nothing would. There was no argument that could move him from his consuming determination to realize the dream of Pakistan.' It seldom happened that Mountbatten's persuasive powers were used in vain, and it is not surprising that he did not like it. Mr Jinnah was probably the only man he had not succeeded in twisting round his little finger. But he fully appreciated his interlocutor's unique importance for the future of India. For he wrote home: 'It was clear that he was the man who held the key to the whole situation.' Yet in these confidential talks there was little of the sympathetic diplomacy of which Mountbatten was so brilliantly capable and which he might have been expected to exercise with special care upon so crucial a figure. The first interview seems to have made an impression that was not dispelled by subsequent meetings. He had found Mr Jinnah 'frigid, haughty and disdainful'.

Looking back at the story of the partition of India, one is beset by a question to which there is no certain answer, because all alternatives in history are only hypothetical, and entirely unpredictable. Was partition the best solution for the future of the people of India after British rule?

To the minds of most British people in 1947, the partition of the subcontinent was a deplorable end to the British Empire. The unity of India, more complete and secure than under any Indian Raj in history, was cause for justified British pride. A strong central government, one system of law ruling throughout, one network of communications and economic relationships, one army to defend a frontier within which peace and order reigned—these were valuable creations which the British felt should be bequeathed to a nation-wide democracy. Up to the last moment of British rule, when Mountbatten and Attlee took the fateful decision to divide the subcontinent, partition seemed to most of the British an evil to be averted at almost any cost. But now, from a greater distance in time, we can perceive that task as short-sighted, and a too self-centred political view. Once, a hundred years ago, the whole subcontinent had been brought under one land; but the land was alien and alien rule, however beneficial, is an intolerable affront to aspirations for national freedom and personal dignity.

Three hundred years ago, when European power was limited to a few parts, most of India was subject to another alien, who sat on the throne of the Mughals. It was already evident that the struggle for mastery between Hindus and Muslims had begun. It continued until the antagonists were eventually separated by an agreement to differ. We can now see with hindsight that the prophets predicting Pakistan's eventual collapse—from lack of economic resources, political experience, or national cohesion—were wrong. These prophets of doom had underrated the emotions that gave rise to the Muslim separatist movement, the sense of national pride and identity that grew with the challenge to its progress, and the vested interest in national power which became a prime motive in those who shared it. Jinnah's Pakistan is now, more than thirty years on, a secure and permanent reality. Its distinct national character and polity give it a rightful, as well as an inevitable, place among the nations of the world.

Lord William Francis Listowel, former Governor-General of Ghana (1957–60), Chairman of the Committee of the House of Lords, served as a Parliamentary Under-Secretary of State for India and Burma during 1944–5 and Parliamentary Secretary of State for India and Burma, 23 April 1947–14 August 1947. Lord Listowel had known the Quaid-i-Azam very closely before partition and had an insight into the Quaid's two-nation theory. Lord Listowel has written a number of books, including *A Critical History of Modern Aesthetics*, and has admirably served as a joint-president, Anti-Slavery Society for the Protection of Human Rights. [Ed.]

4

THE FOUNDER OF PAKISTAN
John Biggs-Davison

I have just been in Pakistan and whenever I go back there people tell me of the inherited British system of administration and I reply: 'Well, the British got it all from the Mughals.' Even in small things, the continuity is evident. I am told that bureaucrats in Britain still fasten papers by means of a green cord with metal tags. I expect some of you are wondering why not the proverbial red tape. The answer is that these metal tags, called Treasury tags, are also known as 'India tags' and were introduced by the old India Office. They were coloured green, whereas the Home Civil Service used red tape until it was abandoned during the 1914 War as an economy. But why green? The best answer that I have been given is that green signified continuity with the Mughal Empire to which the British succeeded.

I am now going to be very provocative and say that it is nothing but racialism to assert that the British title was of less legitimacy than that of their predecessors in conquest.

The Quaid-i-Azam would, I feel, have liked this story about the Treasury tags. He was no enemy of the British Empire. He was also, as previous speakers have told us, a worker for Hindu-Muslim unity and served a political apprenticeship in the Congress. But always he was a constitutionalist, as befitted one who learnt so much within these confines of Lincoln's Inn. He opposed Gandhi's campaigns of so-called civil disobedience. Professedly peaceful, they ended in riots, misery, and death. Maulana Mohammad Ali declared that the Mahatma's movement was 'not for the complete independence of India but for the making of seventy millions of Indian Muslims dependent on the Hindu Mahasabha' [Hindu religious organization]. I would like to balance that statement by saying this: in fairness to the Mahasabha, in 1924 Lala Lajpat Rai himself suggested that India should be partitioned between Hindus and Muslims and Jinnah himself earned the respect of Hindu nationalists.

In 1917 Sarojini Naidu hailed Jinnah as the Muslim Gokhale and the future 'Mazzini of Indian liberation'. But the exemplars and ideology of European liberal nationalism, serviceable to those who sought majority rule in wholly secular and undivided India, had become irrelevant to Muslim fears and hopes. Those fears were fed by the experience of living under Congress ministries after the 1935 Government of India Act, which introduced self-government to the provinces of British India. So much were they oppressed in those days that some Muslim leaders favoured direct action against the Congress rulers.

But, true to form, the Quaid argued—for example at the Patna session of the League in 1938—for patience. In 1939, the expected Second World War began. The Congress ministers resigned rather than support a war declared over their heads. It was a war against aggressive powers and an inhuman ideology which the anti-racist Nehru had denounced. Jinnah called on Muslims to celebrate their deliverance.

It was this experience in 1937–9 which made it clear that when Britain quit India, Britain would have to split India. The experience strengthened adversity, consolidated the Muslim sense of identity. Wilfred Cantwell Smith, the Islamic historian of Forman Christian College, Lahore, and of Aligarh, was no Muslim Leaguer and yet, in a preface written in 1945 to his book *Modern Islam in India,* he pictures a young Muslim in a Lahore coffee-house talking in English of Marx or Lenin. He perhaps never studied the Quran and dislikes what he knows of the canon law and yet he is intensely conscious of being a Muslim. He insists that he and his co-religionists in India are a nation and he is, he says, ready to fight to establish for them a free country.

Although without Gandhi, Hindustan would still have gained independence and, without Lenin and Mao, Russia and China would still have endured Communist revolution, without Jinnah there would have been no Pakistan in 1947. Doubtless it would have emerged later in a bloody revolt against an Indian republic.

Iqbal wrote in a letter to Jinnah on 21 June 1937: 'I remember Lord Lothian telling me before I left England that my scheme was the only possible solution to the troubles in India but it would take twenty-five years to come.' But great wars and great men shorten history. Mountbatten has been mentioned. Mountbatten said, according to the journalists Larry Collins and Dominique Lapierre, that he liked Liaquat Ali Khan (also of Lincoln's Inn) and other Muslim leaders but Jinnah he could not stand. I am reminded of Churchill with de Gaulle. Churchill found de Gaulle a trial, his cross of Lorraine, but if you have a weaker hand to play, then you must play it without throwing any cards away and neither de Gaulle nor Jinnah did that.

Mountbatten misread and underestimated Mohammad Ali Jinnah. He was misled by his own frustration. He was confronted by another aristocrat, cultured, aloof, monocled, immaculate, restrained. The Quaid made an elegant contrast to what he called the Hindu revivalist, Gandhi. He detested demagogy.

By dying tragically so soon, Quaid-i-Azam proved what Pakistan lost. He gave the watchword, 'unity, faith, discipline', which your Society observes and emblazons.

I respectfully offer my congratulations for this inspired initiative and wish you great success as the years go on. 'Whatever you may be,' the Quaid said, 'and whatever you are, you are a Muslim, you have carved out a territory, a vast territory. It is all yours. It does not belong to a Punjabi or Sindhi or a Pathan. There is white too in the lovely flag of Pakistan. The white signifies the non-Muslim minorities.'

'These are exciting days in the history of Pakistan. A new constitution, a new parliament are awaited.' Anticipating an earlier constitution, the Quaid said, 'it would be of a democratic type, embodying the essential principles of Islam...we have many, many Muslims, Hindus, Christians, and Parsees but they are all Pakistanis. They will enjoy the same rights and principles as any other citizens and will play their rightful part in the affairs of Pakistan.'

If a Christian may say it, with respect, anything less would be unIslamic and would dishonour the memories we keep. According to Allama Iqbal, 'the ultimate fate of a people does not depend so much on organization as on the word and power of individual man'. You have the example and justly cherish the glory of one individual man.

Mohammad Ali Jinnah was always chivalrous and courteous. On Christmas Day, in 1947, which was his birthday, he dined with the Royal Scots, a regiment about to sail home. The Commanding Officer announced that he would keep the tradition of the Officers' Mess that there would be no toasts other than those of the Princess Royal, who was their Colonel-in-Chief, and of the King. 'We consider ourselves good fighters,' the Colonel of the Royal Scots said, 'and we consider you, Your Excellency, to be a good fighter too.' The Quaid-i-Azam responded: 'Gentlemen, may I further break the tradition of your regiment and reply: I shall never forget the British who have stayed in Pakistan to help us begin our work. This I shall never forget.'

Nor shall we ever forget him!

Sir John Biggs-Davison was a Conservative Member of Parliament from 1974 until his death in 1990. He retired from the Indian Civil Service in 1948 having served in both India and Pakistan during 1946–8. He co-founded the Pakistan Society in 1951. During and after the transfer of power to the newly created Dominion of Pakistan, he was Deputy Commissioner, Dera Ghazi Khan in 1947. He served the Pakistan Administrative Service ably in 1948. Sir John was the author of many books and contributed to many periodicals. [Ed.]

Mohammad Ali Jinnah with Jawaharlal Nehru and Liaquat Ali Khan, London, December 1946

Mohammad Ali Jinnah with Liaquat Ali Khan, Sardar Baldev Singh, and Lord Pethick-Lawrence at London airport, December 1946

5

JINNAH'S CHARISMA
Viqarunnisa Noon

This was sprung on me and at first I said 'no', but now, having heard these very inspiring speeches, let me also come and address you for just a few minutes and add another side to what kind of a person Mr Jinnah really was.

Being a woman, I wanted you to know that he was most supportive of the status of women. He was absolutely determined to see that women would take their rightful place next to men, a fact which has hardly ever been mentioned.

I would also like you to know that this was the reason for his sister always being at his side, whenever he went anywhere officially, to show that women were equal to men and must take their rightful place. That is very important to remember.

I was a young girl when I met Mr Jinnah. We had many arguments and he was very charming to me in explaining everything. He always tried to convince young people. He loved young people because he felt they were the future of Pakistan.

He took an immense amount of trouble whenever I wrote to him. I would like you to know that this great leader at that time did not impress me as much as I should have been impressed. He answered every letter and I am very proud to be in possession of photocopies of my letters to him and his to me.

I would like you to know also one other very important fact. Mr Jinnah did not know about or envisage the terrible carnage that was going to occur after partition and I have proof of that. I had a small house in the Kulu valley, a district which is in India today. My husband told him that this was a very lovely place. We knew that the area was going to be in India because it was eighty-five per cent Hindu. But Mr Jinnah was ready to acquire some property there and I have correspondence between him and myself regarding this property which he knew was going to remain in India.

We thought and he thought that it was going to be an amicable division and nobody was going to kill anybody. He thought it was going to be something like Canada and the USA. I do not know why some people do not take into consideration that Mr Jinnah did not realize what was going to happen, and it certainly did not happen because Mr Jinnah either gave any encouragement to that kind of thing or even envisaged it. I think that it is very important and we must never forget that.

Just to end, I would like to repeat what Lord Listowel said that Mr Jinnah was very informal when you met him informally in his house. That is quite correct. When Mr Jinnah came to see my husband, who was a Muslim Leaguer even though he was a member of the Viceroy's council, they had much contact. I had the great privilege of knowing him as a young girl. He was very charming to me and very informal. Some people describe him as a cold and distant person. That was not true. He was humane, delightful and understood, at least, my feelings. So I leave you with that thought.

Lady Viqarunnisa Noon (Nishan-i-Pakistan) was a Minister of State, Government of Pakistan. She served as Chairperson of the Pakistan Tourism Development Corporation. Her late husband, Malik Firoze Khan Noon, was Prime Minister of Pakistan in 1958. She knew the Quaid-i-Azam since her late husband was a member of the Viceroy's executive council. [Ed.]

6

A UNIQUE LEADER
Bernard Budd

There is something I think you must know and that is that ninety per cent of the inspiration behind this movement must be ascribed to Mr Saleem Qureshi, and really it is from his lips that you should hear what the purposes of the Society and its offshoot, the Jinnah Academy, are. But he has insisted, and Mr Qureshi is a very persistent gentleman, that I should say a very few words about the Jinnah Academy which is proposed because it is in that area I have been asked to assist.

The idea behind the Academy has been touched on by several of our speakers this evening. There is far too little known about the legal side of Mohammad Ali Jinnah's life, particularly his training here and later his practice before the Privy Council. By any measure, the Quaid-i-Azam was a most unusual man, perhaps untypical of his origins, and I think the historian and the patriot of Pakistan equally would feel it important to analyse in due course the factors that created the character that we have been hearing about. It is with this point particularly in mind, the legal influences that fell on his career, that the Jinnah Academy is proposed. Its main original purpose, although this may be quickly completed, is to dig up as many facts as we can as to what happened during first his pupilage, his training period, and, later his period of practice in the Courts. But then there is much else which could well be done. In the process of research into his legal history, we would discover those issues, those legal issues perhaps, which he took particularly to heart and which he perhaps never had time to complete examination and propagation of, and we would seek, I think, to pursue those issues particularly in relation to the Pakistan of today.

But this is all in the future. We feel that an institution of this kind needs to be built on a firm foundation and we are investigating, in correspondence with the Jinnah Academy of Pakistan, the best legal basis of an institution of this kind. Then, when it has been set legally in motion, work will begin and the progress of this institution will be reported steadily to meetings of the QEAMAJ Society. I hope you will all prod us into action and make sure that progress is genuinely being made.

Bernard Budd, QC, was Deputy Secretary, Ministry of Finance and Works, Government of Pakistan in 1947. He served as an anti-corruption officer, Inspector General of Prisons, and Collector and District Magistrate, Karachi 1945. After being called to the Bar by Gray's Inn in 1952, he was active in the Association of Liberal Lawyers from 1978–82. In 1983, he served as Acting Chairman of the Steering Committee of the M.A. Jinnah Academy. [Ed.]

7

A MAN OF INTEGRITY

Ahmed E.H. Jaffer

As time is running short, I will say only a few words based on my personal experiences with the Quaid-i-Azam. As you know, the Quaid-i-Azam had settled in London in 1931. Sir Mohammad Iqbal and the leaders of Sindh, who came for the Round Table Conference, appealed to him to return to India to lead the Muslims, who were living like orphans without a leader. Quaid-i-Azam was gracious enough to accept the invitation and returned to Bombay in 1934 to contest the elections for the Central Legislative Assembly from the city which he had represented on many occasions before. He contested the election. One thing I must tell you about the Quaid-i-Azam is that he never went to the voters to beg for votes. He only sent out a letter saying, 'You know me, you know my service, and I appeal to you for your vote if you think I am a good representative.' People used to vote for him whilst he sat in his house.

In this election, one Mr Hussain Bulaji of Bombay opposed him and he filed nomination papers against me as well. He did so not because he had any hope of being elected from my constituency, because it was a Muslim League constituency and he was not a

Muslim Leaguer, but with the hope of bargaining for the seat which
I was contesting. He went to the Quaid-i-Azam and said: 'Sir, I
have come with a proposal: I withdraw my candidature against your
seat—you come in unopposed. Ask Jaffer to withdraw and allow
me to come in on that seat.' The Quaid-i-Azam said: 'Get out of
here. Do you think I am going to bargain with you for my personal
benefit? I would rather be defeated but I will not tell Jaffer, the
Muslim League candidate, to withdraw against you.'

In this election we had two seats for the Central Assembly for
the province of Bombay. The elections were fought on non-party
basis. The Quaid-i-Azam and all Muslim candidates, including my
humble self, contested as independent candidates. When we went
to Delhi for the Assembly session [the budget session] in January
1935, there was no Muslim parliamentary party in the central
legislature of India.

The Quaid-i-Azam formed an independent group and then an
independent party. In those days, he was staying in Delhi with
party members. My quarters were next to his. I used to meet Jinnah
practically every day. As I was an independent candidate, I voted
against him on several occasions. One day he invited me to ask me
why I voted against the party, knowing full well that was against
the interest of India. I said, 'Sir, I have an election conviction
against me.' 'What for?' he asked. I said, 'I contested and won the
election soon after I left college at the age of twenty-three while
the minimum age was twenty-five. I was told by leading politicians
before I left Bombay to please the British and be on their right side,
otherwise Lord Willingdon, the then Governor-General of India—
your friend and also a friend of my father—would appoint a
committee for criminal inquiry and throw me out' (which
ultimately happened). He said, 'Look my boy, I will give you one
piece of advice; never do anything against your conscience. If your
conscience says the Government of India is right, vote for them. If
you think I am right, vote for me and my party, but never vote
from the personal consideration that you want a contract or some
payment from government.'

Another thing I would like to tell you about Jinnah. Some speakers have referred to the fact that he was a man of great honesty and integrity. In the 1945 elections which were fought on the basis of the Pakistan Resolution, the candidates contested on Muslim League tickets. The Quaid-i-Azam had appealed to the Muslims of India that even if a Muslim League candidate was a lamppost, vote for the lamppost. People listened to him and voted as he said. Muslims of the minority provinces particularly returned candidates on the Muslim League ticket, both for the provincial and central Assembly.

 Jinnah was a man of great integrity. Whenever he rose to speak in Parliament, his speech was heard with rapt attention on all sides, the Government ministers, the non-officials, and the press. The galleries were full whenever he spoke.

The Quaid-i-Azam was the best-dressed man in Parliament. Once I asked him, 'Sir, there are rumours that your shirts are sent to Paris for washing.' He replied, 'Absolute nonsense.'

The Quaid-i-Azam was a man of his word. He used to tell us, 'If ever you make a promise, think a hundred times, but once you make a promise, honour your promise,' and this is what he always did.

In 1948, the Olympic Games were being held in London. A friend of mine, F.M. Kazmi, and I went to the Quaid-i-Azam and said, 'Sir, the Olympic Games are being held in London. Do not you think that Pakistan should participate?' He liked the proposal very much. He said, 'Go ahead, I want to see the flag of Pakistan flying high among the comity of nations.' In July 1948, some of you may remember that I brought a party of eighty boys. We received several promises from him that he would help us to send the boys to London, to finance them and also to take an interest in and patronize sports and be a patron-in-chief. He honoured all his promises. He entertained the athletes to a garden party in the Governor-General's house to which he invited the whole Cabinet. He was not a sportsman himself but he took a keen interest in sports. In Delhi he had joined the local golf club because he wanted to start playing golf. Later on he bought the club but he could never find the time to go anywhere near it. He sacrificed his health for the cause of the nation, for the sake of Pakistan.

One of the speakers referred to the question of minorities in Pakistan. The Quaid-i-Azam once said, 'You should not only be fair and just to the minorities but generous.' I am proud to say that today the minorities in Pakistan—the Christians, Parsees, Hindus—are all enjoying life as free citizens of a free country. On only one occasion in 1948, during the time of Liaquat Ali Khan, was there a protest opposite the Indian High Commission in Karachi. The Quaid-i-Millat, Liaquat Ali Khan, went there and took the mike, got into a jeep, and told people who had gathered near the exhibition ground, 'Are you going to blacken our faces? The Quaid-i-Azam had given an assurance that we would be fair, just, and generous to our minorities.' They all went away. And look at what is happening today to the Muslims in India. Look at what she [Indira Gandhi] is doing about the Commonwealth. I know many of our friends here want us to return to the Commonwealth. Whatever decision was taken under the circumstances, the fact is that all the Commonwealth countries want Pakistan to return to the Commonwealth except that great lady. Lord Listowel will remember that when he addressed the Commonwealth Society three years ago, I put that question to him. Sir John Biggs-Davison came to Karachi as did Baroness Young. They all said they wanted Pakistan to return to the Commonwealth but why should one country have a veto in the Commonwealth? I hope the other Commonwealth countries will have the courage to stop India opposing Pakistan's entry into the Commonwealth.

I wanted to say more but I do not have much time. I want to congratulate Mr Qureshi for forming this Society which was long overdue. I hope you will hold many functions. We are going to organize Quaid-i-Azam lectures in Pakistan through the English-Speaking Union of Pakistan and we are going to invite leaders. We are very grateful to Sir John Biggs-Davison, Sir Frederick Bennett, and others who visit us frequently. I hope Lord Listowel will honour his promise that he made three years ago that he would come as we are going to hold the silver jubilee celebrations of the English-Speaking Union in January 1985. I invite all of you to come.

Mr Ahmed Ebrahim Haroon Jaffer was a member of the Central Legislative Assembly in India and was India's youngest parliamentarian. He was a close associate of the Quaid-i-Azam, and served on the working committee of the All-India Muslim League. He was a member of the Constituent Assembly of Pakistan and President of the English-Speaking Union of Pakistan. [Ed.]

8

A TRIBUTE
Ali Arshad

It is indeed a matter of great privilege and honour for me to be asked to preside over this function which is the inaugural meeting of the Quaid-i-Azam Mohammad Ali Jinnah Society. As prayer time has approached already, I shall be very brief in my remarks.

Barrister Qureshi and his colleagues deserve to be congratulated on this auspicious occasion. I do hope that they will keep up their efforts and continue to increase the membership of this Society, making it more and more active as time goes by. On behalf of our Embassy, I sincerely offer all help and co-operation to the Society.

Your Society, Barrister Qureshi, should hasten to establish close links with the Quaid-i-Azam Academy in Pakistan, which can offer useful assistance in the important task you have set yourselves.

It will also be worthwhile, I think, to remain in touch with some of the universities in Pakistan which are doing useful research on the Quaid-i-Azam and the history of his period. I also believe that you should organize symposia and seminars and your members should keep on organizing meetings, not only in London but also in other cities.

I had planned to say something about the life of the Quaid-i-Azam but unfortunately the constraints of time prevent me from doing so. However, I would like to refer to one important aspect of the Quaid-i-Azam's character, to which reference has been made in the preceding speeches. This relates to his uprighteousness and honesty. A Muslim officer of the Indian Civil Service, who was working in a Hindu majority province as Secretary to the Chief Minister, came into possession of a document addressed to his boss by some Hindus, in which a plan had been hatched to kill Muslims and to drive them out of the province. The officer, being a Muslim, was shocked to see this document which had come to his notice only because he was in a sensitive and important job. Shocked at the discovery, he rushed to Delhi where the Quaid was staying at that time. He sought an urgent interview with the Quaid and was finally ushered into his presence. There he produced the document, hoping for a pat on the back. The Quaid calmly read the document and then turning to him said: 'You have been guilty of violating the confidence of your boss. You should not have brought this confidential document to me. Instead, if you were deeply concerned about it, you should have taken it to your boss and expressed your honest views about it. Now take this back and do not ever do such a thing again.' Since the matter had come to his attention, the Quaid took necessary steps to rectify the situation and protect the Muslims in this case. But so deep was his sense of honesty and fair play that he would not accept even such valuable information without chiding the officer concerned for his part in violating a trust placed in him.

Let us hope, dear friends, that like our Quaid-i-Azam we shall learn to be straightforward, honest, and upright. For that, in essence, is an important message of Islam.

Ali Arshad was Ambassador for Pakistan in the UK until January 1987. He joined the foreign service in 1948 and held diplomatic assignments in the Pakistan missions in Cairo, 1949–52; New York 1953–6; New Delhi, 1956–8; Tokyo 1960–3; Ghana, 1968–71; and Iran, 1979–80. He was Foreign Secretary, 1972–4. [Ed.]

9

OBITUARY

From *The Times*, 13 September 1948

MR M.A. JINNAH CREATOR OF PAKISTAN

The death on Saturday of His Excellency Mohammad Ali Jinnah, Governor-General of Pakistan, at the age of 71, deprives that Dominion of the Quaid-i-Azam ('Great Leader') by whose exertions, backed by the overwhelming weight of Indian Muslim opinion, it came into being. In addition to holding the Governor-Generalship, he was president both of the Pakistan Constituent Assembly and the Muslim League, which he had made the instrument of his dominance. He ranked with Gandhi and Pandit Nehru in the influence he wielded in the controversies over the shaping of the constitutional destiny of the Indian peoples, both during and after the 1939–45 war. He voiced with authority and skill the Muslims' fears of permanent Hindu domination in any unitary plan and their consequent 'two nations' theory, which ultimately prevailed. By a strange irony of fate Jinnah had been regarded in his early manhood as a stalwart opponent of social or religious particularism, and that great nationalist, G.K. Gokhale, gave him the title of 'The Ambassador of Hindu-Muslim Unity'; Mrs Sarojini Naidu wrote an enthusiastic biography under that title (1918).

Jinnah was born in Bombay[1] on Christmas Day, 1876, being the eldest son of a hide dealer of Karachi. He came to this country for education in 1892, joined Lincoln's Inn, and was called to the Bar. Returning to Bombay[2] in 1896, he was faced with unexpected poverty owing to the financial ruin of his family. After three years of great hardship, he was enrolled at the Bombay High Court, and his abilities soon brought him a large practice. He was private secretary to Dadabhai Naoroji, the 'Grand Old Man of India', when he went from this country to preside at the 1906 session of the National Congress. On the introduction of the Morley-Minto Reforms. in the autumn of 1910, Jinnah was elected to represent the Muslims of the Bombay Presidency in the Viceroy's Legislative Council. In 1913 he joined the recently created All-India Muslim League.

In 1916 he was president of the Bombay Provincial Conference and later of the Bombay branch of Mrs Besant's India Home Rule League. As president of the Muslim League session at Lucknow in 1916 Jinnah had a large share in planning the Lucknow Pact, whereby the Congress and the League reached a settlement of outstanding controversies, but it failed to bring permanent peace and fell into desuetude. In 1919 Jinnah was one of the members of the Imperial Legislative Council who resigned as a protest against the passing of the Rowlatt Acts, but when the Montagu-Chelmsford Reforms were introduced in 1921, he was elected to the Legislative Assembly. He was averse to civil disobedience, and after Mr Gandhi had gained control of the Congress machinery he broke away from that organization. In the Legislative Assembly elected in 1926 there were, apart from the nominated and Government group, five parties. His leadership of one of these, the Independents, enabled him to hold, on occasion, the balance of power, and to dictate his terms, whether to government or the army, and he was a member

---

1. He was born in Karachi. [Ed.]
2. He returned to Karachi and moved to Bombay later. [Ed.]

of the committee which in 1926–7 recommended the setting up of an Indian Sandhurst. He also served on the Reforms Inquiry Committee of members of the Central Legislature in 1923–4.

Jinnah associated himself with the boycott of the Simon Commission and with the All Parties Conference held in Bombay in the spring of 1928. A committee of the conference formulated the famous Nehru report, outlining a plan for Dominion status, but passing lightly over obvious difficulties. At a subsequent meeting of the conference, Jinnah put forward his well-remembered 'Fourteen Points' as constituting the Muslim claims to adequate safeguards in the shaping of further constitutional reforms. They were rejected by the conference but enthusiastically confirmed by the most representative gathering of Indian Muslims ever held, which took place at Delhi on 1 January 1929, under the chairmanship of the Aga Khan. Jinnah was a delegate to the successive sessions of the Indian Round Table Conference in London. In the many attempts made to bring about agreement on safeguards for the minorities, he stood doggedly by his 'Fourteen Points' and settlement was not reached.

Feeling that he was out of tune with prevalent opinion in India, and telling his friends that he had 'no political future there', Jinnah decided to settle in London for practice at the Privy Council Bar and in the hope of gaining a seat in Parliament 'to fight India's battle'. This mood was of short duration, however. He was induced in 1934 to take up the permanent presidentship of the All-India Muslim League. The Congress Party now found in this erstwhile comrade a resourceful opponent. The League rapidly advanced in influence and in membership, for in Northern India at least it vied with the Congress in mass adhesions. Momentum was given to the movement by the coming in 1937 of Congress Cabinet's allegations that the Cabinets were using their powers to the serious detriment of Muslim and other minority rights and interests. The League followed Jinnah's guidance implicitly, though there were men of standing and repute who were critical at times. At the Lucknow session of the League in 1937 Jinnah secured an alteration in the creed, favouring full independence of India in the form of a federation of free democratic States, with full safeguards for minorities. In fact, from the autumn of 1938, a new and positive doctrine was instilled into Muslim minds by the League leader. It was that of separate nationhood entitling the followers of the Prophet to their own 'national homelands' in those areas of north-west and north-east India in which they were in a majority: they must be consolidated into a coherent Muslim State or States by the federation of their component provinces, with such adjustments of their frontiers as might seem advisable. Then Pakistan, of which the poet Sir Mohammad Iqbal had dreamed, became the watchword of millions of Muslims throughout India.

The demand for Pakistan coloured subsequent discussions on the constitutional issue. The invitation of Lord Linlithgow in August 1940 for Jinnah to join with other political leaders in a reconstituted Executive Council at Delhi was met by the claim that all the Muslim nominees should be drawn from League adherents; and a like attitude was taken to subsequent efforts by Lord Wavell to set up an interim National Government.

There is no need to trace in detail the prolonged negotiations of the two main parties of the subcontinent which finally led to the creation of the two Dominions. In the discussions with Sir Stafford Cripps's mission in 1942, in those with the Labour Government's mission of 1946, and in all the subsequent negotiations and party manoeuvring, Jinnah played a predominant part. The situation was finally brought to a head by Mr Attlee's announcement to Parliament in February 1947 of the intention of His Majesty's Government to withdraw every vestige of British authority by June 1948 and that Lord Wavell was retiring and being replaced by Lord Mountbatten. The latter, sworn in at the end of March, applied forcing tactics. He brought the warring parties to agree to compromise solutions which both had declared impossible of acceptance. It was agreed to establish the separate Dominion of Pakistan, but the price reluctantly paid by Mr Jinnah was that of depriving Pakistan of those portions of the Punjab and Bengal predominantly non-Muslim in population, the boundaries to be determined by an impartial British arbiter of high forensic repute.

The settlement was rushed through and came into being under the India Independence Act ten weeks after its terms had been announced, with many long-debated issues to be dealt with in subsequent discussions. It had been the wish of Lord Mountbatten to be Governor-General of both Dominions and in that he was a mediating influence; but the Quaid-i-Azam—now the Pakistan title for Jinnah—was nominated to the office by the Karachi Government. Thus Jinnah had none on a higher level to confer with. He gave instructions to, rather than took the advice of, his Ministers. He was immediately confronted by the unparalleled outbreak of communal bloodshed in the Punjab, with the consequent migration of millions of terror-stricken people—the Muslims into Pakistan, and the Hindus and Sikhs from thence into East Punjab. The new Pakistan administration, starting from zero (in contrast to the great modern capital city and the working administrative machine inherited by Mr Nehru's Government) had to devote primary attention to the immediate necessities of the refugees, to the neglect of other pressing claims. Then came the disputes with New Delhi regarding the employment of India Government troops in Kashmir and the small Kathiawar State of Junagadh. Concentration of final authority in the Quaid-i-Azam not only held up urgent decisions but also imposed so severe a strain on that septuagenarian that his health broke down and he had to spend much time in retirement in Balochistan.

Jinnah provided a striking contrast to Mahatma Gandhi. He lived in stately mansions, was tall and elegantly groomed, with a distinguished presence and fastidious tastes. In his fast-greying hair a white lock stood aggressively like a plume. Jinnah owed much of his later success to the impression he made upon Western investigators of the Indian communal problem; for he provided in his own person the best illustration of his contention that the Muslims constitute a separate nation. There was nothing in him of the subtle flexibility of intellect which seems to the Englishman characteristic of the Hindu; all his ideas were diamond-hard, clear-cut, almost tangible. His arguments had none of the sinuosity of Hindu reasoning; they were directed, dagger-like, to the single points he was attacking. He was a formidable antagonist. The clear, cold courage which was the counterpart of his arrogance impelled him along his chosen course without a thought for the feelings of his opponents. His remarkable command of invective enabled him to be outrageously insulting in debate; but he was not thin-skinned, and was ready to take hard knocks as well as to give them.

Jinnah went outside the Islamic fold for a wife by marrying a daughter of Sir Dinshaw Petit, the Parsee baronet.[3] She died after a dozen years or so of married life, leaving a daughter, who married the son of Sir Ness Wadia, a Parsee by birth and a Christian by conversion. A devoted unmarried sister, Miss Fatima Jinnah, was his chatelaine.

3. This statement is incorrect. According to Professor Sharif-al-Mujahid, Ruttenbai had embraced Islam on 18 April 1918 at City Jamia Masjid at the hands of Maulana Nizam Ahmad Khajandi and married Jinnah on 19 April 1918. See Sharif-al-Mujahid, *Quaid-i-Azam and His Times*, Islamabad: Quaid-i-Azam Academy, 1990, vol. 1, 1876–1937, p. 36. [Ed.]

10

LEAD ARTICLE
The Times, Monday, 13 September 1948

To the people of Pakistan the death of Mr Jinnah brings the same sense of personal loss that the people of India felt at the passing of Mr Gandhi. The two men were very different, but each embodied in himself the national hopes of millions. Mr Jinnah was something more than Quaid-i-Azam, supreme head of state, to the people who followed him; he was more even than the architect of the Islamic nation he personally called into being. He commanded their imagination as well as their confidence. In the face of difficulties which might have overwhelmed him, it was given to him to fulfil the hope foreshadowed in the inspired vision of the great Iqbal by creating for the Muslims of India a homeland where the old glory of Islam could grow afresh into a modern State, worthy of its place in the comity of nations. Few statesmen have shaped events to their policy more surely than Mr Jinnah. He was legend even in his lifetime.

To Mr Jinnah himself, his legend was cause for sardonic amusement, but he knew the strength it gave him. The somewhat cynical detachment which he cultivated all through his career puzzled both friends and foes. It was thus that he freed himself

Mohammad Ali Jinnah giving interview to *Life* magazine, Karachi, 1945

Lord Wavell greets Mohammad Ali Jinnah upon his arrival for discussions with the Cabinet Mission. Also present are Lord Pethick-Lawrence (left), A. V. Alexander (middle), and Sir Stafford Cripps (right), March 1946

from the deadening routine of administration. He had few illusions. He knew that, although he had himself largely fixed the hour and circumstance of the birth of Pakistan, he was director and not creator of the forces that made Pakistan possible. He knew that his work would not last unless he taught his people to be independent of his guidance, and more and more he gave over the responsibilities of government to the band of able men he had collected and trained. He stood in the background to give the people confidence, and to step in decisively when the hour required it. It is thus as presiding genius rather than as active statesman that Mr Jinnah's loss will be most deeply felt. No succeeding Governor-General can quite fill his place, for as the 'father of the nation' his prerogatives were enlarged by popular acclaim far beyond the limit laid down in the Constitution. Now those whom he trained to responsibility will carry the burden in their own right; they will leave the shelter of his name and seek their own ways of achieving the ideals he taught them. They have been well trained, but they take over at a critical moment. Their country is beset with perilous anxieties in its relations with its neighbour. Great ideas of popular passion over the Kashmir dispute have been whipped into a tempest over the fate of Hyderabad, which now hangs in the balance.

There has been no moment since the two Dominions first came into existence when calm and courageous statesmanship was more needed. Two of the makers of independence, Mr Gandhi and Mr Jinnah, are dead; the third, Mr Nehru, has the fate of their work in his hands. Invasion of Hyderabad by Indian forces might plunge the whole continent into disaster. However the Government of India justifies to itself the action which it now contemplates against Hyderabad, resort to force will not be excused. In Kashmir it is argued by the Government of India that the ruler's right to accede to India brings Kashmir within the Indian union; the right of the Nizam of Hyderabad to choose freely, unfettered by force or pressure, cannot be denied. It is within the power of Mr Nehru to choose the way of peace. There can be no doubt of the course which his guide, the dead Mahatma, would have chosen.

© *Times Newspapers Limited 1948*

JINNAH
A RETROSPECTIVE VIEW

11

A GREAT CONSTITUTIONALIST
Gordon Johnson

It is a great privilege to have been invited to your inaugural meeting. I would not say very much because it is appropriate that we should hear from those who know more about the subject than I do.

I was a child when Mr Jinnah died and Pakistan was founded. In fact I am the sort of person for whom this Society is founded, and I hope we can look to the Society as an organization which will help promote our understanding not only of Mr Jinnah, but also of Pakistan and its position in the world.

I must admit as an historian that there is a great difficulty about Mr Jinnah, and the difficulty is this: he was not a great writer of letters and diaries, he did not have fleets of secretaries around him taking down every word he said and, in a curious way, he was a very private man who lived a perfectly normal life such as any successful barrister from Lincoln's Inn would do. And the result is that there is a great scarcity of source material about Mr Jinnah and, in particular, about those crucial closing years from the mid-1930s onwards.

We historians are bound to get Gandhi wrong because there is so much of Gandhi that whatever we look for we can find. We are almost, and I hope Lord Listowel will forgive me here, bound to get the British story wrong, despite the fact that we have now twelve volumes of documents on the transfer of power in India. These reveal the muddles and inconsistencies and the sheer difficulties of the whole job.

Although we might be able to construct some sort of narrative from them, it is perfectly clear that there is still a lot that we do not know and can never know. Now with Mr Jinnah we are likely to get him wrong because we do not know enough. So, of course, we will clutch at straws, remembrances of things that may or may not have happened in his youth. We will hold on to the reminiscences of those who knew him, which may be embroidered with the passage of time, and we will seek to judge him by what we believe he did rather than by what he did.

There is one thing that the previous speakers have all referred to that gives us hope in our enterprise. And that is this: Mr Jinnah was a lawyer, and he was the great constitutionalist. Everybody has stressed that. But the importance of that fact is that he knew you had to get the constitution right—it was no good just having any constitution because the constitution provides the legal framework of society.

Unless you get that framework right, there is room for iniquity and inequality to operate throughout society. I think that looking at the history of the Indian subcontinent in the twentieth century, the thing that worried him most was that the main development in the Indian State was towards a federal structure of some sort, but a federal structure that had entrenched in it a very powerful, or potentially very powerful, central government.

It was not a government that would only look after foreign affairs, communications, and defence. It was a government that could actually interfere, if it wished to, quite legally and constitutionally, across the whole range of social activity. And so it was, although the 1920 Montagu-Chelmsford Reform and, more importantly, the 1935 Government of India Act did establish self-governing provinces in British India, there was always the threat that without adequate legal constitutional safeguards built into the central government, whoever was able to command a majority in the centre would be able to interfere with the lives, the culture, and society of those who were in the provinces.

This is why the great Muslim leaders, particularly in the Punjab and also in Bengal, began to realize after 1935 that perhaps the way in which the Indian Constitution should be developed was one in which the central government would be much weaker—a more simply co-ordinating body.

And in a way that is what the demand for Pakistan was all about. A particularly well-organized and important minority interest in India wished to secure a future for itself within the new government.

In the end, as we all know, this led to a total partition. I think that if we look closely at the history of the time, the partition was not necessarily inevitable. It was perhaps not necessarily what Mr Jinnah himself wanted because he was a great mediator.

Reference has been made to his earlier work in the Congress and he was a great mediator between the Muslim politicians of India— between the Punjabis and people from the UP and the people from the Frontier and Bengal, and from Sindh and Balochistan. And so the creation of this State, which was a very important landmark in the twentieth century, can be seen, I think, almost in terms of good, old-fashioned constitutional law, and in terms of a political development in India which expressed itself in a legal way.

What I am saying to you is that it will be hard to study Mr Jinnah. It will be hard to find enough source material, although a lot is being produced particularly by the Academy in Pakistan now, and we await, of course, the major biography of Mr Jinnah from that Academy. Much more material needs to be sought out, and I think that your Society, Mr Qureshi, will need to look at the political developments of the twentieth century in a very general way and not just at the social, cultural, and political development of Muslims only.

As Sir John Biggs-Davison pointed out, Mr Jinnah did not work for an exclusively Muslim State. He really believed that in his Pakistan there would be room for minorities who would, of course, be good Pakistanis also.

Mr Jinnah was a very great leader. Without him Pakistan would not have appeared, certainly in the form in which it did and at the time it did. Now that the trauma of partition has receded into the past, so that you can have many people in this hall who were but barely born when it happened, perhaps we should try to see how Mr Jinnah's contribution to our political life in the twentieth century can be made more general.

He set a great example to other statesmen to follow by his skill at negotiation, his integrity, and his honesty. So I wish the Society very well and I hope it prospers here in Lincoln's Inn and I hope, too, that it attains your main objectives.

Dr Gordon Johnson has been Director, Centre of South Asian Studies since 1983. He was a Fellow of Trinity College, Cambridge 1966–74, and has been a Fellow of Selwyn College, Cambridge since 1974. He was a Joint Chairman of the Oxford and Cambridge working party on the future of Oriental Studies in the two universities (1982–3). He has been Chairman, Committee of Management of the Centre of Middle Eastern Studies since 1989; Editor of *Modern Asian Studies* (Cambridge University Press Quarterly) since 1971; and Chairman, Editorial Board, Cambridge, *South Asian Studies* since 1983. Dr Johnson is an eminent writer and author of several books on the Third World, South Asia, and India. [Ed.]

12

FOUNDER OF A NEW NATION
Alexander Andrew Mackay Irvine

A MESSAGE FROM THE LORD CHANCELLOR
ON THE OCCASION OF THE LAUNCH
OF SALEEM QURESHI'S BOOK

Not many people found a new nation; I can think of Bismarck and George Washington—Cecil Rhodes is perhaps another. But the situations which confronted them were very different from what Jinnah faced. Recently we have seen many new nations formed as a result of the collapse of communism but the prospective fractures which led to the creation of so many new smaller states had only been concealed by authoritarianism. On the other hand the Indian subcontinent had been an entity (perhaps 'an idea') for thousands of years, including people of the same ethnic and cultural origins.

To have exerted so much influence and leadership that not only the British Government, but also in the end the Congress Party of India, had to concede the case for partition, was heroic effort. No wonder Jinnah earned the title Quaid-i-Azam, the Great Leader. Yet if we now ask the man in the street question, who were the leaders of the independence movement in India, Gandhi would be mentioned, but few would remember Jinnah. Mr Qureshi's book will correct this.

The founder of modern Turkey, Kemal Ataturk, specifically established a secular estate, although with a Muslim population. Pakistan was created at the insistence of the Muslim League to ensure that those of the minority Muslim faith would not be oppressed by a Hindu majority. I doubt, however, whether Jinnah would have supported any trend towards an Islamic state. His instincts were more international. The comparison with Gandhi's appearance was significant.

The fiftieth anniversary of the death of Jinnah was only a few weeks ago. Sadly he outlived the birth of Pakistan by only just over a year. Mr Qureshi's work is timely.

It is specially pleasing for me, a fellow barrister turned politician, to associate myself with the tributes paid to another barrister turned politician. Mohammad Ali Jinnah was not a member of my Inn*, but I know how proud Lincoln's Inn is that he was one of their members. Mr Qureshi's work does justice to a man of history as well as acknowledge the influence of the English legal system on his later career.

*Jinnah was called *ad eundem* by the Inner Temple: 5 May 1931

The Right Honourable The Lord Irvine of Lairg of the Honourable Society of the Inner Temple—The Lord High Chancellor of England and Wales 1997–2003.

JINNAH
AND
IQBAL

13

IQBAL'S LETTERS TO JINNAH

JINNAH AND IQBAL

Although in the western world Iqbal is known as a poet, he was an eminent politician who guided, and was highly respected by Jinnah.

Jinnah held him in such esteem that on the anniversary of Iqbal's death he said, *'If I am given a chance to choose between the work of Iqbal and a future Islamic state, I will choose Iqbal's work'*.

When the correspondence from Iqbal to Jinnah was published in book form in 1942* Jinnah wrote the foreword in which he said, *'I think these letters are of very great historical importance, particularly those which explain his views in clear and unambiguous terms on the political future of Muslim India. His views were substantially in consonance with my own and had finally led me to the same conclusion as a result of careful examination and study of the constitutional problems facing India and found expression in due course in the united will of the Muslim India as adumbrated in the Lahore resolution of the All India Muslim League, popularly known as the 'Pakistan Resolution' passed on 23 March 1940'*.

---

* *Letter of Iqbal to Jinnah*, Sh. Muhammad Ashraf, Lahore 1942.

Reproduced here are the following three extracts:
1. Letter dated 28 May 1937
2. 21 June 1937
3. 7 October 1937

Confidential

Lahore
28th May, 1937

My dear Mr. Jinnah,

Thank you so much for your letter which reached me in due course. I am glad to hear that you will bear in mind what I wrote to you about the changes in the constitution and programme of the League. I have no doubt that you fully realise the gravity of the situation as far as Muslim India is concerned. The League will have to finally decide whether it will remain a body representing the upper classes of Indian Muslims or Muslim masses who have so far, with good reason, taken no interest in it. Personally I believe that a political organisation which gives no promise of improving that lot of the average Muslim cannot attract our masses.

Under the new constitution the higher posts go to the sons of upper classes; the smaller ones go to the friends or relatives of the ministers. In other matters too our political institutions have never thought of improving the lot of Muslims generally. The problem of bread is becoming more and more acute. The Muslim has begun to feel that he has been going down and down during the last 200 years. Ordinarily he believes that his poverty is due to Hindu money-lending or capitalism. The perception that it is equally due to foreign rule has not yet fully came to him. But it is bound to come. The atheistic socialism of Jawaharlal is not likely to receive much response from the Muslims. The question therefore is: how is to possible to solve the problem of Muslim poverty? And the whole future of the League depends on the League's activity to solve this question. If the League can give no such promises I am sure that Muslim masses will remain indifferent to it as before. Happily there is a solution in the enforcement of the Law of Islam and its further development in the light of modern ideas. After a long and careful study of Islamic Law I have come to the conclusion that if this system of Law is properly understood and applied, at last the right to subsistence is secured to everybody. But the enforcement and development of the Shariat of Islam is impossible in this country without a free Muslim state or states. This has been my honest conviction for many years and I still believe this to be the only way to solve the problem of bread for Muslims as well as to secure a peaceful India. If such a thing is impossible in India the only other alternative is a civil war which as a matter of fact has been going on for some time in the shape of Hindu-Muslim riots. I fear that in certain parts of the country, e.g. N.-W. India, Palestine may be repeated. Also the insertion of Jawaharlal's socialism into the body-politic of Hinduism is likely to cause much bloodshed among the Hindus themselves. The issue between social democracy and Brahmanism is not dissimilar to the one between Brahmanism and Buddhism. Whether the fate of socialism will be the same as the fate of Buddhism in India I cannot say. But is clear to my mind that if Hinduism accepts social democracy it must necessarily cease to be Hinduism. For Islam the acceptance of social democracy in some suitable form and consistent with the legal principles of Islam is not a revolution but a return to the original purity of Islam. The modern problems therefore are more easy to solve for the Muslims than for the Hindus. But as I have said above in order to make it possible for Muslim India to solve the problems it is necessary to redistribute the country and to provide one or more Muslim states with absolute majorities. Don't you think that the time for such a demand has already arrived? Perhaps this is the best reply you can give to the atheistic socialism of Jawaharlal Nehru.

Anyhow I have given you my own thoughts in the hope that you will give them serious consideration either in your address or in the discussions of the coming session of the League. Muslim

India hopes that at this serious juncture your genius will discover some way out of our present difficulties.

Yours sincerely,
(Sd.) Muhammad Iqbal

P.S. On the subject-matter of this letter I intended to write to you a long and open letter in the press. But on further consideration I felt that the present moment was not suitable for such a step.

Private and Confidential

Lahore
June 21st, 1937

My dear Mr. Jinnah,

Thank you so much for your letter which I received yesterday. I know you are a busy man; but I do hope you won't mind my writing to you so often, as you are the only Muslim in India today to whom the community has a right to look up for safe guidance through the storm which is coming to North-West India, and perhaps to the whole India.

Yours sincerely,
(Sd.) Muhammad Iqbal
Bar-at-Law

Lahore
7th October 37

My dear Mr. Jinnah,

A strong contingent from the Punjab is expected to attend the Lucknow session of the League. The unionist Muslims are also making representations to attend under the leadership of Sir Sikander Hayat. We are living in difficult times and the Indian Muslims expect that your address will give them the clearest possible lead in all matters relating to the future of the community.

JINNAH
AND
LINCOLN'S INN

14

ALMA MATER

The following extract is reproduced with thanks from the
handbook *An Introduction to Lincoln's Inn*
by Sir Robert Megarry

In the heart of central London lies Lincoln's Inn, a haven from
the roar of traffic and crowded pavements. The Inn occupies
most of the rectangle formed by High Holborn on the north, Carey
Street and the Royal Courts of Justice on the south, Chancery Lane
on the east, and Lincoln's Inn Fields on the west. Indeed, if one
excludes the frontage to High Holborn and the south-eastern block,
the eleven acres of the Inn comprise virtually all that remains. The
Inn is old, very old: but it is no mere relic. It houses a living,
functional body of public importance, the Honourable Society of
Lincoln's Inn. 'Lincoln's Inn' is thus a term which describes both
the place and the Society which inhabits it. Before looking at the
place, something may be said about the Society.

THE INNS OF COURT

Lincoln's Inn is one of the four Inns of Court. The Inns of Court
are ancient unincorporated bodies of lawyers which for five

centuries and more have had the power to call to the Bar those of their members who have duly qualified for the rank or degree of Barrister-at-Law. In modern times, much of the process of education for call to the Bar and of discipline has been carried out by joint bodies of the four Inns; but the four Inns—Lincoln's Inn, Inner Temple, Middle Temple, and Gray's Inn, to put them in their customary order—remain distinct, as friendly rivals, each with its own property, duties, and functions.

ORIGINS

Lincoln's Inn is ancient. Its formal records, contained in the 'Black Books', go back continuously to 1422. This is nearly eighty years earlier than any other Inn. It is plain, too, that in 1422 the Inn had been in existence for some while. There is some ground for saying that an Ordinance of Edward I made in 1292 was in some part responsible for the founding of the Inns. The Ordinance placed both branches of the profession (barristers and solicitors, as they would be called today) under the control of the judges, and hastened the end of the clergy as lawyers in the King's Court; and the new race of professional lawyers that began to emerge needed places where they could congregate and where apprentices could be housed.

Whatever their origins, the Inns, when established, came to provide all that was needed for practice at the Bar. There were Chambers to live and work in, a hall to eat and drink in, a chapel or church to pray in, and a library to consult books in.

MEMBERSHIP

The three ranks of membership of the Inn are students, barristers, and benchers. The lowest rank, that of student (once known as 'inner barrister'), is open to all of good character who satisfy certain educational requirements which nowadays include acceptance by a British university for a degree course. On obtaining a degree, passing during the four dining terms of the year (a process which can usually be completed in about a year), the student qualifies for

call to the Bar. The process of formal education and examination
for the Bar has for over a century been carried out by the Council
of Legal Education on behalf of the four Inns. But Lincoln's Inn
plays a full and vigorous part in supplementing this process by
means of moots and debates and by a system of sponsorship
whereby practising barristers give general assistance to students on
an individual basis. Call to the Bar is made by the Treasurer of the
Inn on one of the four call days in the year. The student then
becomes a barrister, or as it was once called, an 'outer' or 'utter'
barrister.

BENCHERS

The highest rank of membership is that of the benchers, or (more
formally) the Masters of the Bench. These provide the governing
body of the Inn, meeting periodically as a body in Council. There
are over 130 ordinary benchers, elected for life by the Council.
They all pay a substantial sum into the funds of the Inn on
election. It is customary to elect as benchers all members of the Inn
appointed to all judicial office, most practising Queen's Counsel of
more than six or seven years' standing in silk, i.e. those who have
been QCs for this length of time, and some seven or eight of the
most distinguished practising 'juniors' of the Inn, i.e. those
barristers (whatever their age) who have not become QCs. In
addition, a small number of the Inn who, though not practising at
the Bar, have attained important positions in their walks of life have
been elected 'additional benchers' with all the rights and duties of
ordinary benchers except that they cannot hold office in the Inn.
There are also some thirty honorary benchers who have all the
privileges of ordinary benchers save that they can neither vote nor
hold office. Any person of sufficient distinction may be elected an
honorary bencher, despite not being a member of the Inn or even
a lawyer.

OFFICERS OF THE INN

The Inn has five honorary officers. The Treasurer is the head of the Inn. There are also the Master of the Library, the Dean of the Chapel, the Keeper of the Black Book, and the Master of Walks. The normal course is for a bencher to hold each office for a year starting with the most junior and progressing to Treasurer. Most of the detailed work of the Inn is done under delegated powers by some twenty committees and a number of sub-committees, subject to the confirmation of any decision of major importance by the Council. Some of the committees include members of the Inn who are not benchers. The Inn also employs a permanent staff, headed by the Under Treasurer and his Deputies.

TOPOGRAPHY

The heart of the Inn is the central section, with the Old Hall, the Chapel and the Gate House on the east, and the Great Hall, the Library, and the offices on the west. Old Square, Old Buildings, and Hale Court are also in the area, on the east. At the north is Stone Buildings and at the south is New Square.

THE OLD HALL

The Old Hall is the finest building in the Inn and, indeed, is one of the finest buildings in London. It is small but beautifully proportioned and executed. In addition to discharging the functions of the dining-hall of the Inn, the Old Hall was also regularly used as a Court of Justice. This first occurred in 1717, when the Master of the Rolls sat there during the rebuilding of his Court on the east side of Chancery Lane, on a site now forming part of the Public Record Office. The Old Hall again came into use when Lord Talbot, the Lord Chancellor, sat there in 1733; and from 1737 onwards it was in regular use as the High Court of Chancery out of term time.

Entrance to Lincoln's Inn

A view of the Great Hall of Lincoln' Inn

THE GREAT HALL

By the beginning of the nineteenth century the Old Hall was becoming inadequate for meeting all the demands made upon it; and the membership of the Inn was increasing apace. The foundation stone of the Great Hall (or New Hall) was laid on 20 April 1843. In a state ceremony, Queen Victoria opened the hall on 30 October 1845.

The Great Hall now serves all the normal purposes of a hall in an Inn. During the four dining terms of the year, each twenty-three days long, it is used for dining, and students of the Inn keep their terms there. In addition, the hall provides lunches for members throughout the year, and the social and professional fellowship that this affords is an important facet of life at the Bar.

Much of the life of the Inn centres round the Great Hall. It is there, four times a year, that the formal ceremony of calling students of the Inn to the Bar takes place. In the presence of a number of other benchers and of friends and relations of those concerned, the Treasurer says to each student in turn, 'Mr A.B., by the authority and on behalf of the Masters of the Bench I publish you a barrister of this Honourable Society.' With those simple words the student becomes a barrister, and what may be a distinguished career in law has begun. New benchers, too, are published in a similar way at lunch-time when the hall is full. During the dining terms, there are a number of moots or debates for students, or talks by well-known lawyers.

THE LIBRARY

The present library building stands at the north end of the Great Hall. It is approached by the staircase which also leads to the Benchers' Rooms; and beneath the library are the offices of the Inn. All these structures were built at the same time as the Great Hall, in 1843–5, though the library was extended eastwards in 1872. Before the present building was erected, the library was at No 2 Stone Buildings; and before 1787 there was a library close to the Old Hall. As a collection of books, the library has been in continuous existence for five centuries. Until 1777, the more valuable books were secured by chains. In addition to law reports, statutes, legal textbooks, and all the usual material of a working law library, there are many other books on a wide range of subjects, including topography, local records, parish registers, and many branches of literature.

THE GATE HOUSE

Until the Great Hall was built in 1843–5 and the present main entrance from Lincoln's Inn Fields on the west was constructed, the principal way to the Inn was from Chancery Lane on the east through the Gate House entrance. The Gate House itself was built during the years 1517–21, with bricks dug and made within the Inn. There are grounds for saying that Ben Jonson worked as a bricklayer on the Gate House and the wall that divided the Inn from Chancery Lane.

PAINTINGS

Of the many paintings in the Inn, some are very fine. At the north end of the Old Hall, above the place where the Lord Chancellor used to sit, hangs Hogarth's vast canvas (10 feet by 14 feet) of Paul Before Felix (based on Acts, c 24.)

In the Great Hall, the whole of the upper part of the plaster of the north wall is occupied by the enormous fresco by G.F. Watts, OM, RA. The painting, some 45 feet wide by 40 feet high, is entitled *Justices, A Hemicycle of Law-givers*.

Also in the Great Hall, hanging on the eastern side, is an oil painting by Norman Hepple, RA, entitled *Short Adjournment*. It commemorates the occasion when six out of the nine members of the Court of Appeal were benchers of the Inn; and it shows them as they might have been seen any day after lunch in the Benchers' Drawing Room, wearing court dress but no robes. While the painting was in progress, one of the six was elevated to the House of Lords and became Lord Denning; but in his place another bencher of the Inn was appointed (now Lord Pearce), and so the painting includes all seven figures with that of Lord Denning appropriately in motion towards the door.

In 1979 the Treasurer, Lord Renton, commissioned a corresponding portrait by William Dring, RA. This commemorates the fact that the Prime Minister, Mrs Margaret Thatcher MP, the Lord Chief Justice of England, Lord Widgery, the Master of the Rolls, Lord Denning, and the Vice Chancellor, Sir Robert Megarry, were all benchers of the Inn.

CHAMBERS

Much of the Inn consists of four- or five-storey buildings, with the top floor or floors used as residential flats and the rest used as professional chambers or offices. The names displayed at the entrance to each staircase will usually reveal how each floor is occupied. A bare list of names, often eight or ten or more, signifies a set of barristers' chambers; by custom QCs and juniors alike appear as plain 'Mr'.

There are three main groups of such buildings: Stone Buildings to the north, New Square to the south, and in the centre a complex consisting of Old Square, Old Buildings, and what is now Hale Court. For several centuries this complex, together with the Old Hall and the chapel, contained all the buildings of the Inn. But the premises of the Inn were then extended in three waves of building: southwards by New Square in 1682–93; northwards by Stone Buildings in 1775–80; and westwards by the Great Hall and library in 1843–5. The twentieth century brought lesser additions: Hale Court (1967–9); Erskine Chambers, 30 Lincoln's Inn Fields, in the north-west corner of the Inn (1989); and Hardwicks Building (1990) on the site of the disused seventeenth century Boghouse (or House of Office) to the east of Numbers 1–3 New Square. Hale Court was built in 1967–9, and at the same time Numbers 22–24 Old Buildings were extensively reconstructed. Apart from that, the general body of the old buildings was erected over the period 1524–1609. The numbers today run from 16–24, with Numbers 16–18 ranged in an order that defies reason. The stonework bearing the Numbers 25 and 26 was preserved during the reconstruction of Numbers 22–24, but now frames windows rather than doorways. Of the earlier numbers, only 1 remains, with its entrance in the northern segment of the Gate House. Much of what is now known as Old Square, with numbers running from 8–15, stands on what used to be part of Old Buildings and was erected between 1872 and 1887.

Lincoln's Inn is the home of an active society of barristers and judges, who live out a large part of their professional lives within its walls. The Inn does much to enable them to function efficiently, and at the same time to work and relax in a tranquil environment. It is the Inn which, like the other Inns, makes it easy for the Bar to exemplify Tranio's advice:

Do as adversaries do in Law
Strive mightily, but eat and drink as friends.

Right Honourable Sir Robert Megarry, PC, of Lincoln's Inn, Barrister, QC; Bencher Lincoln's Inn, 1962, Treasurer, 1981; High Court Judge, 1967–85; Vice Chancellor, High Court Chancery Division, 1976–81; Vice Chancellor, Supreme Court, 1982–5; Reader, 1967–71, in Equity in the Inns of Court; Member, Faculty of Law, University of Cambridge, 1939–40; Director, Law Society Research Courses, 1944–7; Visiting Professor, New York University School of Law, 1960–1; Sir Robert is also the author of several books on the law of real property. [Ed.]

A view of the library of Lincoln's Inn

Portrait of Mohammad Ali Jinnah hanging in the Great Hall of Lincoln's Inn

15

RECORD BOOKS— LINCOLN'S INN LIBRARY

1. MEMBERSHIP RECORDS

Membership records of Lincoln's Inn are fairly complete for the entire period 1422 to the present. A Register of Admission has been printed covering the period 1422 to 1973, reconstructed for the period 1422 to 1573 from lists in the Black Books, and thereafter from the separate 'Calendar' ordered to be kept on 21 June 1574:

> A Kalendar shall be made for those which hereafter shall be admitted into this House and of their keeping the exercises of Ierninges.

By 1990 this Register occupied forty-one volumes, and was kept contemporaneously with the dates of admission by the Chief Butler until 1767, thereafter by the steward (alias Under Treasurer) and his staff. From 1573 until 1589 the order to record Learning Exercises was obeyed in the back of the same volume, together with various memoranda and orders concerning the butlers, food and drink, and payment of dues.

The first volume in this class is not an Admission Register, but is simply a chronological list of members, compiled retrospectively from 1558 in the early seventeenth century, again by the Chief Butler, and updated at intervals until 1865. Its purpose was presumably as a quick guide to precedence, and as a sort of index. It indicates only names and years of joining the Inn. It was clearly intended to be a permanent record, being the only surviving parchment volume among the Inn's archives.

The form of description has changed from time to time. The earlier entries only give the name of the person admitted. In 1440, the first mention of the parentage of the person admitted occurs, one Stanshaw 'Le Tierce' is mentioned as having as surety his father, Nicholas Stanshaw. Like entries occur for the most part when the father was a member of the Inn. About 1608, it becomes the ordinary practice to mention the father's name; in 1612, the description 'son and heir' marks the eldest or only son, and a few years later persons admitted are described as second or third sons, as the case might be. After 1563 the country of origin is generally mentioned, and in 1805 the age of the student is first included in the entry of the admission. Persons described as Barristers of the Inn or Chancery first appear among the admission in 1573.

An important function of the early Admission Books was financial: each admission entry was made, but also by one, two, or three sureties or manucaptors. These were members of the society who had proposed the new member, and who were bound to ensure his payment of dues to the Society. If a member later changed his manucaptors, the new ones signed an agreement in the back of the Admission book.

Manucaptors are frequently named in admission entries in the Black Book from November 1539. From that date, the entries become a short set form; earlier entries vary as to the amount of detail. During the seventeenth century the practice becomes less strict; noblemen, for example, being excused the duty of providing sureties, and the custom was dropped altogether in 1767. Thereafter, a brief marginal note is made of a 'Bond given' (a few of which survive).

Sureties' names have not been transcribed into the printed Admission Register, although they are of great interest. Superficially, the Admission Registers prior to 1757 become an indexed autograph collection. More importantly, they are a prime source for the study of political and social alliances in Elizabethan and Jacobean society (together with Admission to Chambers for the same period, which are similarly unindexed).

Admission Registers covering this period 1573 to 1627 contain various memoranda and orders ignored by the editor of the Admissions. These are therefore noted at some length in this list.

The statutory abolition of Latin and court-hand for legal business in 1733 is reflected in the Register of Admission then in use. On a single page are contrasted one entry in Latin and a legal hand with another written in English in a round hand.

The Admission Register of Lincoln's Inn continues to be handwritten, although it has not been signed by any admitting Bencher since 1910.

The records kept for Mr Jinnah, his admission entry, and his call to the Bar, have been recorded in a similar fashion to those recorded for centuries.

Lincoln's Inn is very aware of its responsibility to preserve records and retain current ones for future historians. The older records have been catalogued and safely stored. Documents which need conservation are given expert care and older records are kept under strict temperature and humidity control.

2. Bar Books

Call to the Bar has been recorded independently of the Black Books only since 1767. Part of the reformed office practice introduced by the new Steward, Thomas Grint, the list was back-dated to 1757. From 1767, however, those called have signed their names (unless called in absence during the late nineteenth and twentieth centuries). The entries have included the names of the proposing Bencher and of the Benchers present at the call since Hilary 1792. Stamp duty was paid on Call to the Bar until Hilary 1947; entries in the Call Books were therefore stamped. Each volume is separately indexed.

[Courtesy, The Librarian, Lincoln's Inn]

16

OFFICIAL DOCUMENTS—
LINCOLN'S INN ARCHIVES

Among the archives of the Lincoln's Inn Library are the original documents, dated between April 1893 and April 1896, relating to Jinnah's studies, some of which are in his own handwriting. Thirteen of the documents are reproduced on the following pages with kind permission of the Library:

1. Application for dispensation from test in Latin

2. Cover of Lincoln's Inn Record of Admissions Book

3. Entry in the Lincoln's Inn Register

4. Letter to the British Museum from R.H. Smith, recommending a seat for Jinnah in the Reading Room

5. Note from Jinnah to the Librarian at the British Museum

6. Note (reply) from Jinnah to the Librarian giving the reason for his request for a seat in the Reading Room

7. Note from the British Museum

8. Declaration regarding age

9. Application to amend name

10. Petition for call to the Bar

11. Declaration of eligibility for call to the Bar

12. Motion by Graham Hastings for Jinnah's call to the Bar

13. Jinnah's petition for a Certificate of call to the Bar

14. Entry in the Bar Book for Jinnah's call

APPLICATION FOR DISPENSATION FROM TEST IN LATIN

London 25th April 1893.

To:

The Masters of the Bench of
The Honourable society of Lincoln's Inn

Sirs

    I most humbly & respectfully, beg to inform you that I intend to appear for the preliminary Exam

    Having learnt that I shall be examined in the Latin Language I request you in this petition to grant me dispensation for the following reasons.

    I Being a native of India I have never been taught this language.

    II. I know several of Indian languages which we are required to learn as our Classics or second languages.

    III Thus having spent my time in learning other languages which are required there I have not been able to learn the Latin Language & which if I be compelled to learn will take some years to pass the required exams

    I hope you will kindly comply with my request considering the reasons to be satisfactory

I remain sirs
Yours most humble & obedient
servant
Mahomedalli Jinnahbhai
40 Glazbury Road
West Kensington
W.

APPLICATION FOR DISPENSATION FROM TEST IN LATIN

London 25th April 1893

To:
    The Masters of the Bench of
    The Honourable Society of Lincoln's Inn

Sirs

I humbly & respectfully beg to inform you that I intend to appear for the preliminary Exam.

Having learnt that I shall be examined in the Latin Language I request you in this petition to grant me dispensation for the following reasons.

I Being a native of India I have never been taught this language.

II I know several of Indian languages which we are required to learn as our classics or second languages.

III Thus having spent my time in learning other languages which are required there I have not been able to learn the Latin language & which if I be compelled to learn will take some years to pass the required exam.

I hope you will kindly comply with my request considering the reasons to be satisfactory.

I remain sirs
Yours most humble & obedient servant
Mahomedalli Jinnahbhai
40 Glazbury Road
West Kensington W.

COVER OF LINCOLN'S INN RECORD OF ADMISSIONS BOOK

THE

RECORDS OF THE HONORABLE SOCIET

OF

Lincoln's Inn.

VOL. II.

ADMISSIONS

FROM

A.D. 1800 to A.D. 1893,

AND

CHAPEL REGISTERS.

LINCOLN'S INN.
—
1896.

ENTRY IN THE LINCOLN'S INN REGISTER

444   𝕷𝖎𝖓𝖈𝖔𝖑𝖓'𝖘 𝕴𝖓𝖓 𝕬𝖉𝖒𝖎𝖘𝖘𝖎𝖔𝖓 𝕽𝖊𝖌𝖎𝖘𝖙𝖊𝖗 : 1420–1893.

1893   May   9   HAROLD WALTER MARIGOLD, of Trin. Coll., Camb., B.A., a student of the Honorable Society of the Inner Temple (admitted 6 Oct., 1890), 3 s. James M., late of Birmingham, Warwickshire, solicitor, decd.

"   9   ARTHUR ROBERT INGPEN, a barrister of the Middle Temple (admitted 10 Aug., 1876, called 17 Nov., 1879), LL.B., and of the London Uny., son of Robert Frederick I., of 95, Chancery Lane, Esq.

"   29   JOHN FREDERICK BADGER MOODY, of Exeter Coll., Ox. (28), the eldest son of John M., late of Derby, co. Derby, solicitor, decd.

"   30   GEORGE DUNSTAN TIMMIS, B.A., of Ch. Ch. Coll., Ox. (27), 2 s. Thomas Sutton T., of Allerton, co. Lancashire, manufacturer of chemicals.

"   30   SYED ALI AUSAT, of the Uny. of Allahabad, India (22), the only son of Syed Mahdi Ali, of Meerut, Division of Meerut, North Western Provinces of India, Government servant.

"   31   TRIBHOVANDAS MANEKCHAND DOSHI, of Elphinstone Coll., Bombay (19), the eldest son of Manekchand Tulshi, of Rajkote, Bombay, India, State Minister.

June   2   SHEIKH SHAMSUDDIN, of Christ's Coll., Camb. (18), the only son of Sheikh Amiruddin of Allahabad, North West Provinces, India, bar.-at-law.

"   5   MAHOMEDALLI JINNAHBHAI, of Karachi, India (19), 1 s. Jinnahbhai, of Karachi, Sind, India, afsd., merchant.

"   6   BAVAMIA ABAMIA SHAIKH, of Mangrol, in Kathiawar, India (20), 3 s. Abamia Shaikh, late of Mangrol, afsd., decd.

"   15   RICHARD OSWALD MILLS, of the Uny. of London (23), the eldest son of Richard M., of the Exchequer and Audit Department, Somerset House, London, Esq., C.B., Assistant Comptroller and Auditor-General.

Oct.   2   DHAN RAJ SHAH, of Jhelam, Punjab, India (20), the son of Fogir Chand, of Jhelam, in the Punjab, afsd., late Munsiff.

"   9   EGBERT GEORGE RAND, B.A., of Christ's Coll., Camb. (25), 2 s. John R., of Dulwich, co. Surrey, surgeon.

"   11   ALFRED BARRETT NUTTER, of Brasenose Coll., Ox. (23), the only son of John Frederick N., of Caldwell Priory, Bedford.

"   12   LIONEL TUDWAY LEVICK, of Pembroke Coll., Ox., Undergraduate (20½), 7 s. James L., of Sydney, co. Cumberland, New South Wales, merchant.

"   18   GOOLAMHOOSEIN FAZHULBHOY VISRAM, of the Uny. of Bombay (18), 2 s. Fazhulbhoy Visram, of Bombay, a Member of the Governor General's Legislative Council.

LETTER TO THE BRITISH MUSEUM FROM R.H. SMITH

To the Principal Librarian
British Museum

[stamp: BRITISH MUSEUM 7 JAN 1895 No. 249]

Sir, I beg to state that
I am acquainted with
Mr. M. A. Jinnah of
Lincolns Inn, Student
at Law, and feel sure
that he will make a
proper use of the Reading
Room. if he is admitted
as a reader

                    Yrs faithfully
                    R.V. Smith
            4 Stone Buildings
                Lincolns Inn
            & 116 Welbourne Terrace
7 Jan. 1895. Bayswater W

LETTER TO THE BRITISH MUSEUM FROM R.H. SMITH

To The Principal Librarian
British Museum

Sir,

I beg to state that I am acquainted with M. A. Jinnah of Lincoln's Inn, student at law, and feel sure that he will make a proper use of the Reading Room if he is admitted as a reader.

Yours faithfully

4 Stone Buildings
Lincoln's Inn
116
7 Jan. 1895   Barrister-at-Law

NOTE FROM JINNAH TO THE LIBRARIAN

Sir,

I beg to enclose herewith a letter of recommendation and beg to inform you that I seek admission to the Reading Room for references etc.

NOTE (REPLY) FROM JINNAH TO THE LIBRARIAN

35 Russell Road
Kensington

Sir,

I beg to reply [to] yours that my <u>particular </u>object for admission to the Reading Room is for <u>references </u>generally and especially to some oriental works.

My private address at present is above.

Hoping you will oblige me by sending the ticket to the Common Room, Lincoln's Inn.

Yours faithfully,

M.A. Jinnah

FROM THE BRITISH MUSEUM

A.53227

No. *249*

Jan. 10. 2. 95

Bᴜʀɪᴛɪsʜ Mᴜsᴇᴜᴍ,

9 Jan, 1895.

The Principal Librarian of the British

Museum begs to inform _____ *Mr.*

_____ *M. Alli Jinnah*

Ahomed

that a Reading Ticket will be delivered to

him on presenting this Note to the

Clerk in the Reading-room, within Six

Months from the above date.

N.B.—*Persons under twenty-one years of age*

are not admissible.

FROM THE BRITISH MUSEUM

A. 53227 Jan. 10.2.95

No. <u>249</u>

BRITISH MUSEUM

<u>9 Jan., 1895</u>

The Principal Librarian of the British Museum begs to inform <u>Mr Mahomed Alli Jinnah</u> that a Reading Ticket will be delivered to <u>him</u> on presenting this Note to the Clerk in the Reading-room, within Six Months from the above date.

N. B. *Persons under twenty-one years of age are not admissible.*

W B & L (x)–51462-5000-10-94

DECLARATION REGARDING AGE

I have read the "DIRECTIONS respecting the Reading Room,"
And I declare that I am not under twenty-one years of age.

I have read the "DIRECTIONS respecting the Reading Room,"
And I declare that I am not under twenty-one years of age.

I have read the "DIRECTIONS respecting the Reading Room,"
And I declare that I am not under twenty-one years of age.

DECLARATION REGARDING AGE

A 53227

I have read the 'DECLARATIONS respecting the Reading Room,'

And I declare that I am not under twenty-one years of age.

M.A. Jinnah
35 Russell Road
Kensington

APPLICATION TO AMEND NAME

35 Russell Rd
Kensington
W
30th March 96.

To The Steward
Lincoln's Inn

Sir, I beg to inform
you that I am desirous of
dropping the ending of my name
namely bhai — meaning Mr.
as I explained to you. It being
customary in India at the time
of my admission. I happen to
give the name after that
fashion. I shall feel much
obliged if you can and will
alter it without it causing
you any great inconvenience
the name should be M. A.
Jinnah or in full
Mahomed Alli Jinnah

Hoping you will
See that it is altered
at any rate before
my call.

Yours faithfully
M. A. Jinnah

APPLICATION TO AMEND NAME

Alb/1896, April 14.

35 Russell Road
Kensington

30th March 96

To

The Steward
Lincoln's Inn

Sir,

I beg to inform you that I am desirous of dropping the ending of my name, namely bhai—meaning Mr—as I explained to you. It being customary in India, at the time of my admission, I happened to give the name after that fashion. I shall feel much obliged if you can and will alter it without causing you any great inconvenience. The name should be M.A. Jinnah and in full Mahomed Alli Jinnah.

Hoping you will see that it is altered at any rate before my call.

Yours faithfully
M.A. Jinnah

PETITION FOR CALL TO THE BAR

Petition and Declaration for Call to the Bar.

Petition.

Lincoln's Inn   Easter Term, 1896

To The Worshipful Masters of the Bench,

The Petition of Mahomed Alli Jinnah (Admitted as Mahomedalli Jinnahbhai) of Karachi India, The First Son of Jinnahbhai of Karachi, Sind, India, aforesaid, Merchant | state condition of life and occupation

Sheweth

That your Petitioner was admitted of this Society on the 5th day of June 1893 and is now desirous of being Called to the Bar, having attained the age of Twenty one years kept Twelve Terms Commons, passed a Public Examination to the satisfaction of the Council of Legal Education, and conformed himself to the Rules of this Society.

moved by Mr Graham Harley

Your Petitioner therefore prays that your Worship will be pleased to Call him to the Bar this Term on paying all his arrears of Commons and Dues with the Customary Fines and Composition to the Treasurer of this Society.

£ 1 ''

And your Petitioner will pray, &c;

(Sign here Mahomed Alli Jinnah

P. T. O

For Declaration see page 3

PETITION FOR CALL TO THE BAR

Petition and Declaration for Call to the Bar

Petition

Lincoln's Inn—Easter Term, 1896

To The Worshipful Masters of the Bench,

The Petition of Mahomed Alli Jinnah (Admitted as Mahomedalli Jinnahbhai) of Karachi India, The First Son of Jinnahbhai of Karachi, Sind, India, aforesaid, Merchant.	State condition of life and occupation.

Sheweth

That your Petitioner was admitted of this Society on the 5th day of June 1893 and is now desirous of being Called to the Bar, having attained the age of Twenty one years kept Twelve Terms Commons, passed a Public Examination to the satisfaction of the Council of Legal Education, and conformed himself to the Rules of this Society.

Your Petitioner therefore prays that your Worships will be pleased to Call him to the Bar this Term on paying all his arrears of Commons and Dues with the Customary Fines and Composition to the Treasurer of this Society.

And your Petitioner will pray, &c;

Mahomed Alli Jinnah

For Declaration see page 3.   P.T.O.

DECLARATION OF ELIGIBILITY FOR CALL TO THE BAR

Declaration

I Mahomed Alli Jinnah (Admitted as Mahomed alli Jinnahbhai) being desirous of being called to the Bar by the Honourable Society of Lincoln's Inn do hereby declare and undertake as follows –

That I am not a person in Holy Orders (or that I, being a person in Holy Orders have not during the year next before the date of this Declaration, held or performed any Clerical preferment or duty, or performed any Clerical functions, and do not intend any longer to act as a Clergyman)

2. That I am not and have never since my admission as a Student of this Honourable Society, been or allowed my name to appear as, an Attorney-at-Law, a Solicitor, a Writer to the Signet, a Writer of the Scotch Courts, a Proctor, a Notary Public, a Clerk in Chancery, a Parliamentary Agent; an Agent in any Court original or appellate, a Clerk to any Justice of the Peace; a Registrar of any Court; an Official Provisional Assistant or Deputy Receiver or Liquidator under any Bankruptcy or Winding-up Act or acted directly or indirectly in any such or similar capacity, or in the capacity of Clerk of or to any of the persons above described, or in the service of any of the persons above described (except as a Pupil in a Solicitor's Office) or as Clerk of or to any Judge, Barrister, Conveyancer, Special Pleader, Equity Draftsman; or Clerk of the Peace; or of or to any Officer in any Court of Justice

3. That I will not, if Called to the Bar, and while and so long as I remain a Barrister, be or act as an Attorney-at-Law, a Solicitor, a Writer to the Signet, a Writer of the Scotch Courts, a Proctor, a Notary Public, a Clerk in Chancery, a Parliamentary Agent an Agent in any Court original or appellate, or a Clerk to any Justice of the Peace, or act directly or indirectly in any such or similar capacity, or in the capacity of Clerk of or to any of the persons above described, or in the service of any of the persons above described, or be or act as Clerk of or to any Judge, Barrister, Conveyancer, Special Pleader, Equity Draftsman; or Clerk of the Peace, or of or to any Officer in any Court of Justice; and that I will not, while and so long as I am, in practice as a Barrister be or act as a Registrar of any Court, or be or act as an Official Provisional Assistant or Deputy Receiver or Liquidator under any Bankruptcy or Winding-up Act, or be or act as Clerk of or to any such Registrar, Receiver, or Liquidator, or act in any such or similar capacity, or be or act in the service of any such Registrar, Receiver or Liquidator

Dated this 21st day of April 1896

Mahomed Alli Jinnah

DECLARATION OF ELIGIBILITY FOR CALL TO THE BAR

I Mahomed Alli Jinnah (Admitted as Mahomed Alli Jinnahbhai) being desirous of being called to the Bar by the Honourable Society of Lincoln's Inn do hereby declare and undertake as follows:-

1. That I am not a person in Holy Orders (or that I, being a person in Holy Orders have not during the year next before the date of this Declaration, held or performed any Clerical preferment or duty, or performed any Clerical functions, and do not intend any longer to act as a Clergyman).

2. That I am not and have never since my admission as a Student of this Honourable Society been or allowed my name to appear as, an Attorney-at-Law, a Solicitor, a Writer to the Signet, a Writer of the Scotch Courts, a Proctor, a Notary Public, a Clerk in Chancery, a Parliamentary Agent, an Agent in any Court original or appellate, a Clerk to any Justice of the Peace, a Registrar of any Court, an Official Provisional Assistant or Deputy Receiver or Liquidator under any Bankruptcy or Winding-up Act, or acted directly or indirectly in any such or similar capacity, or in the capacity of Clerk of or to any of the persons above described, or in the service of any of the persons above described (except as a Pupil in a Solicitor's Office), or as Clerk of or to any Judge, Barrister, Conveyancer, Special Pleader, Equity Draftsman, or Clerk of the Peace, or of or to any Officer in any Court of Justice.

3. That I will not, if Called to the Bar, and while and so long as I remain a Barrister, be or act as an Attorney-at-Law, a Solicitor, a Writer to the Signet, a Writer of the Scotch Courts, a Proctor, a Notary Public, a Clerk in Chancery, a Parliamentary Agent, an Agent in any Court original or appellate, a Clerk to any Justice of the Peace, or act directly or indirectly in any such or similar capacity, or in the capacity of Clerk of or to any of the persons above described, or in the service of any of the persons above described, or be or act as Clerk of to any Judge, Barrister Conveyancer, Special Pleader, Equity Draftsman, or Clerk of the Peace, or of or to any Officer in any Court of Justice, and that I will not while and so long as I am in practice as a Barrister be or act as a Registrar of any Court, or be or act as an Official Provisional Assistant or Deputy Receiver or Liquidator under any Bankruptcy or Winding-up Act, or be or act as Clerk of or to any such Registrar, Receiver, or Liquidator, or act in any such or similar capacity, or be or act in the service of any such Registrar, Receiver, or Liquidator.

Dated this 21st day of April 1896.

Mahomed Alli Jinnah

DECLARATION OF ELIGIBILITY FOR CALL TO THE BAR

Call to the Bar.   Easter Term 1896

I have undertaken to move the Call of Mr Mahomed Alli Jinnah (who was admitted as Mahomedalli Jinnahbhai) at the Special Council appointed to be held at ½ past 5 o'Clock on Friday the 24th of April   1896

Graham Hastings,

To The Steward   Bencher of Lincoln's Inn

Please to Note. That signing this Paper does not supersede the necessity of attending at the Council herein referred to

DECLARATION OF ELIGIBILITY FOR CALL TO THE BAR

Call to the Bar. Easter Term, 1896

I have undertaken to move the call of Mr Mahomed Alli Jinnah (who was admitted as Mahomedalli Jinnahbhai) at the Special Council appointed to be held at 1/2 past 5 o'Clock on Friday the 24th of April 1896.

Graham Hastings

To the Steward   Bencher of Lincoln's Inn

Please to Note that signing this paper does not supersede the necessity of attending the Council herein referred to.

JINNAH'S PETITION FOR A CERTIFICATE OF CALL TO THE BAR

PETITION BY A BARRISTER FOR A CERTIFICATE.

Lincoln's Inn, { *Last day Easter* Term, 189*6*.

To the *Worshipful Masters of the Bench.*

The Petition of *Mahomed Alli Jinnah* of *Karachi, India, The First Son of Jinnahbhai of Karachi, Sind, India, Merchant*

Sheweth,

That your *Petitioner was admitted on the* *Fifth* day of *June 1893* , *and called to the Degree of Barrister-at-Law on the* *29th* day of *April* – 1896 *hath conformed himself to the Rules of this Society, and is now desirous of taking a Certificate of his standing and deportment in this Society.*

Your Petitioner therefore prays that your Worships will be pleased to grant him a Certificate of such his Admission, Call to the Bar, and of his deportment in this Society, on paying all his Arrears of Dues and Duties to the Treasurer within one Month from the date of the Order made hereon; your Petitioner undertaking to pay all Dues hereafter to accrue due from him.

And your Petitioner will pray, &c.

M. A. Jinnah

JINNAH'S PETITION FOR A CERTIFICATE OF CALL TO THE BAR

PETITION BY A BARRISTER FOR A CERTIFICATE

Lincoln's Inn. Last day Easter—Term, 1896.

To the Worshipful Masters of the Bench.

The Petition of Mahomed Alli Jinnah of Karachi, India, The First Son of Jinnahbhai of Karachi, Sind, India, Merchant

Sheweth,

That your Petitioner was admitted on the Fifth day of June 1893, and called to the Degree of Barrister-at-Law on the 29th day of April, 1896, hath conformed himself to the Rules of this Society, and is now desirous of taking a Certificate of his standing and deportment in this Society.

Your Petitioner therefore prays that your worships will be pleased to grant him a Certificate of such his Admission, Call to the Bar, and of his deportment in this Society, on paying all his Arrears of Dues and Duties to the Treasurer within one Month from the date of the Order made hereon; your Petitioner undertaking to pay all Dues hereafter to accrue due from him.

And your Petitioner will pray, &c.
M.A. Jinnah

ENTRY IN THE BAR BOOK FOR JINNAH'S CALL

ENTRY IN THE BAR BOOK FOR JINNAH'S CALL

Proposed by Graham Hastings, Esq.

Published to the Bar by Edward Henry Pember, Esq. Q.C., Treasurer on the 29th day of April 1896 in the presence of

John Westlake, Esq.
George Wirgman Hemming, Esq.
Frank Whittaker Bush, Esq.
Edward Parker Wolstenholme, Esq.
William Phipson Beale, Esq.
              and
David Lindo Alexander, Esq.

Pursuant to Order of Council
        28th April 1896

JINNAH
AND THE
INNER TEMPLE

17

A BRIEF HISTORY

In the middle of the twelfth century, the Military Order of the Knights Templar built a fine round church by the Thames, which became known as the Temple Church. Two centuries later, after the abolition of the Order in 1312, lawyers came to occupy the Temple site and buildings. They formed themselves into two societies, the Inner Temple and Middle Temple, first mentioned by name in a manuscript yearbook of 1388. Interestingly the area on the edge of the site, known as the Outer Temple, did not house a separate legal society.

The medieval Inns of Court, which included Lincoln's Inn and Gray's Inn as well as the Inner Temple and Middle Temple, were recognised on the same basis as the colleges at Oxford and Cambridge Universities, offering accommodation to practitioners of the law and their students and facilities for education and dining. The term 'Inns of Court' seems to have been adopted on account of the hospitality offered to those associated with the law courts. By the end of the sixteenth century, the Inns had largely developed into their present form, governed by an elected Treasurer and Council of benchers, administered by a salaried Sub-Treasurer and his staff.

They called qualified practitioners to the Bar, as barristers with a monopoly to plead in the central law courts. The Inns of Court, which taught English Common Law, developed the three levels of membership still in use today: masters of the Bench (or Benchers), elected from amongst the eminent members of the profession; barristers, qualified to practise on call to the Bar; and Bar students. The Inns also appoint Honorary Benchers, Academic Benchers and Royal Benchers.

The sixteenth century was an age of expansion for the Inner Temple and new buildings were constructed to accommodate its growing membership, although not all the students joining at this time intended to pursue a legal career. The Great Fire of London of 1666 destroyed many of the Inner Temple buildings and a series of subsequent fires and twentieth century war damage were responsible for further losses. The Hall, Treasury Office, Benchers' Rooms and Library were all reconstructed after the Second World War. However, the best preserved chambers buildings in the Inner Temple, which date from the seventeenth century, can be found in the fine terrace at the east end of the site, known as King's Bench Walk after the King's Bench Office which was based there until the nineteenth century.

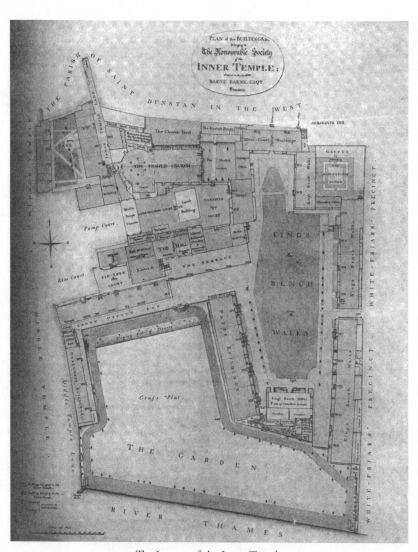

The Layout of the Inner Temple

King's Bench Walk, Inner Temple

18

OFFICIAL DOCUMENTS— THE INNER TEMPLE ARCHIVES

II King's Bench Walk where Jinnah practised

Page from the Rent Book for II King's Bench Walk (Amount deleted where rent paid)

The Record Book containing decisions and orders of the Inner Temple Benchers

Entry in the Bench Table Order Book showing the decision to allow Jinnah to be called *ad eudem* to the Inner Temple

II King's Bench Walk where Jinnah practised

Page from the Rent Book for II King's Bench Walk (Amount deleted where rent paid)

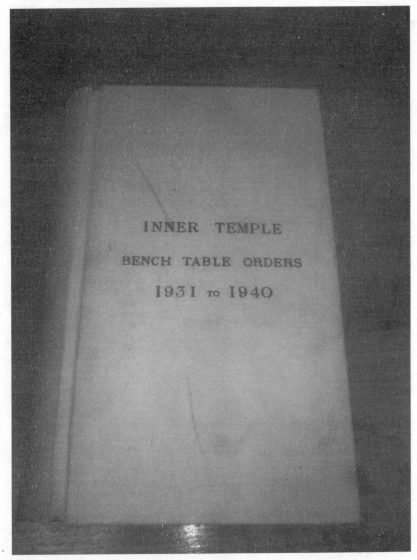

The Record Book containing decisions and orders of the Inner Temple Benchers

Tuesday 5 May 1931.

Bench Table   Tuesday 5 May 1931.
Present

The Treasurer

Mr Bremner   Mr Langdon
Mr Grant   Mr Rolt
Sir D. Kerly   Sir H. Slesser
Mr Bayford   Mr Dunlop
Sir R. Coventry   Mr Goddard
        Mr Beebee

The minutes of the last meeting of the Bench were read but not approved.

Master Langdon having called attention to an omission from the statement of Master Taylor a discussion ensued and it was eventually moved by Master Rolt and seconded by Master Langdon: That there be inserted after the words "Master Taylor resolved to withdraw his candidate" the words "while reserving the right to nominate whom he thought fit hereafter."
This motion was carried and it was Ordered accordingly.

Upon reading an application by Mr M.A. Jinnah, a Barrister of Lincoln's Inn, to be admitted "ad eundem" of this

Entry in the Bench Table Order Book showing the decision to allow Jinnah to be called *ad eudem* to the Inner Temple

Tuesday 5 May 1931.

Society. it was Ordered: That his admission be approved.

It was Ordered: That Master Singleton be, and he is hereby appointed, a member of the Joint Committee on the Duties, Interests and Discipline of the Bar in the place of the late Master Thorn Drury.

The minutes of the last meeting having been altered were then initialled and signed by the Treasurer.

AM Bremner

Bench Table   Friday 8 May 1931.
Present-
                    Mr Bremner
     Sir Lancelot Sanderson   Sir G.F. Hohler

a Parliament

At the Bench Table the minutes of the last meeting of the Bench were read and approved.

Mr P Smitasire (a Student) having paid all dues and requested that his name may be withdrawn from the books of the Inn —

JINNAH'S SPEECHES

19

THE CASE FOR PAKISTAN

Extract from the Quaid-i-Azam's Presidential Address
to the All-India Muslim League, Lahore Session,
22–24 March 1940

We are meeting today in our session after fifteen months. The last session of the All-India Muslim League took place at Patna in December 1938. Since then many developments have taken place. We had many difficulties to face from January 1939 right up to the declaration of war. We had to face the Vidya Mandir in Nagpur. We had to face the Wardha scheme* all over India. We had to face ill-treatment and oppression to Muslims in the Congress-governed provinces. We had to face the treatment meted out to Muslims in some of the Indian States such as Jaipur and Bhavnagar. We had to face a vital issue that arose in that small State of Rajkot. Rajkot was the acid test made by the Congress which would have affected one-third of India. Thus, the Muslim League had all along to face various issues from January 1939 up to the time of the declaration of war. Before the war was declared, the

---

* All-India Congress' drive to establish the superiority of Hindi over Urdu, declaring Urdu the language of the Muslims. [Ed.]

greatest danger to the Muslims of India was the possible inauguration of the federal scheme in the Central Government. We know what machinations were going on. But the Muslim League was stoutly resisting them in every direction. We felt that we could never accept the dangerous scheme of Central Federal Government embodied in the Government of India Act, 1935. I am sure that we have made no small contribution towards persuading the British Government to abandon the scheme of Central Federal Government. In creating that mind in the British Government, the Muslim League, I have no doubt, played no small part. You know that the British people are very obdurate people. They are also very conservative; and although they are very clever, they are slow in understanding. After the war was declared, the Viceroy naturally wanted help from the Muslim League. It was only then that he realized that the Muslim League was a power. For it will be remembered that up to the time of the declaration of war, the Viceroy never thought of me but of Gandhi and Gandhi alone. I have been the leader of an important Party in the Legislature for a considerable time, larger than the one I have the honour to lead at present, the Muslim League Party in the Central Legislature. Yet the Viceroy never thought of me before. Therefore, when I got this invitation from the Viceroy along with Mr Gandhi, I wondered within myself why I was so suddenly promoted and then I concluded that the answer was the 'All-India Muslim League' whose President I happen to be.

I believe that was the worst shock that the Congress High Command received, because it challenged their sole authority to speak on behalf of India. And it is quite clear from the attitude of Mr Gandhi and the High Command that they have not yet recovered from that shock. My point is that I want you to realize the value, the importance, the significance of organizing yourselves. I will not say anything more on the subject.

But a great deal yet remains to be done. I am sure from what I can see and hear that Muslim India is now conscious, is now awake, and the Muslim League has by now grown into such a strong institution that it cannot be destroyed by anybody whoever he may happen to be. Men may come and men may go, but the League will live forever.

Now, coming to the period after the declaration of war, our position was that we were between the devil and the deep sea. But I do not think that the devil or the deep sea is going to get away with it. Anyhow, our position is this: we stand unequivocally for the freedom of India. But it must be freedom for all India and not freedom of one section or, worse still, of the Congress caucus and slavery of Musalmans and other minorities.

Situated in India as we are, we naturally have our past experiences and particularly by our experience of the past two and a half years of provincial constitution in the Congress-governed provinces we have learnt many lessons. We are now, therefore, very apprehensive and can trust nobody. I think it is a wise rule for everyone not to trust anybody too much. Sometimes we are led to trust people but when we find in actual experience that our trust has been betrayed, surely that ought to be sufficient lesson for any man not to continue his trust in those who have betrayed him. Ladies and gentlemen, we never thought that the Congress High Command would have acted in the manner in which they actually did in the Congress-governed provinces. I never dreamt that they would ever come down so low as that. I never could believe that there would be a gentlemen's agreement between the Congress and the Britishers to such an extent that although we cried hoarse, week in and out, the governors were supine and the Governor-General was helpless. We reminded them of their special responsibilities to us and to other minorities and the solemn pledges they had given to us. But all that had become a dead letter. Fortunately, Providence came to our help and that gentlemen's agreement was broken to pieces and the Congress, thank Heaven, went out of office. I think they are regretting their resignations very much. The bluff was called off. So far so good.

I, therefore, appeal to you, in all seriousness that I can command, to organize yourselves in such a way that you may depend upon none except your own inherent strength. That is your only safeguard and the best safeguard. Depend upon yourselves. That does not mean that we should have ill-will or malice towards others. In order to safeguard your rights and interests you must create that strength in yourselves that you may be able to defend yourselves. That is all that I want to urge.

Now, what is our position with regard to the future constitution? It is that, as soon as circumstances permit or immediately after the war at the latest, the whole problem of India's future constitution must be examined *de novo* and the Act of 1935 must go once and for all. We do not believe in asking the British Government to make declarations. These declarations are really of no use. You cannot possibly succeed in getting the British Government out of this land by asking them to make declarations. However, the Congress asked the Viceroy to make a declaration. The Viceroy said, 'I have made the declaration'. The Congress said, 'No, no; we want another kind of declaration. You must declare now and at once that India is free and independent with the right to frame its own constitution by a constituent assembly to be elected on the basis of adult franchise or as low a franchise as possible. This assembly will of course satisfy the minorities' legitimate interests.' Mr Gandhi says that if the minorities are not satisfied then he is willing that some tribunal of the highest character and most impartial should decide the dispute.

Now, apart from the impracticable character of this proposal and quite apart from the fact that it is historically and constitutionally absurd to ask the ruling power to abdicate in favour of a Constituent Assembly—apart from all that, suppose we do not agree as to the franchise according to which the Central Assembly is to be elected, or suppose, we the solid body of Muslim representatives, do not agree with the non-Muslim majority in the Constituent Assembly, what will happen? It is said that we have no right to disagree with regard to anything that this Assembly may do in framing a national constitution of this huge subcontinent except those matters which may be germane to the safeguards for the minorities. So we are given the privilege to disagree only with regard to what may be called strictly safeguards of the rights and interests of minorities. We are also given the privilege to send our own representatives by

separate electorates. Now, this proposal is based on the assumption
that as soon as this constitution comes into operation the British
hand will disappear. Otherwise there will be no meaning in it. Of
course, Mr Gandhi says that the constitution will decide whether
the British will disappear and, if so, to what extent. In other words,
his proposal comes to this: First give me the declaration that we
are a free and independent nation, then I will decide what I should
give you back! Does Mr Gandhi really want the complete
independence of India when he talks like this? But whether the
British disappear or not, it follows that extensive powers must be
transferred to the people. In the event of there being a disagreement
between the majority of the Constituent Assembly and the
Musalmans, in the first instance, who will appoint the tribunal?
And suppose an agreed tribunal is possible and the award is made
and the decision given, who will, may I know, be there to see that
this award is implemented or carried out in accordance with the
terms of that award? And who will see that it is honoured in
practice, because, we are told, the British will have parted with their
power mainly or completely? Then what will be the sanction
behind the award which will enforce it?

We come back to the same answer; the Hindu majority would
do it—and will it be with the help of the British bayonet or Mr
Gandhi's 'ahimsa'?* Can we trust them any more? Besides, ladies
and gentlemen, can you imagine that a question of this character,
of social contract upon which the future constitution of India
would be based affecting 90 millions of Musalmans, can be decided
by means of a judicial tribunal? Still, that is the proposal of the
Congress.

Before I deal with what Mr Gandhi said a few days ago, I shall
deal with the pronouncements of some of the other Congress
leaders—each one speaking with a different voice. Mr
Rajagopalacharya, the ex-Prime Minister of Madras, says that the
only panacea for Hindu-Muslim unity is the joint electorates. This
is his prescription as one of the great doctors of the Congress

---

* Doctrine of non-violence.

organization! Babu Rajendra Prasad on the other hand only a few days ago said, 'Oh, what more do the Musalmans want?' I will read to you his words. He says, referring to the minority question: 'If Britain would concede our right of self-determination, surely all these differences would disappear.' How will our differences disappear? He does not explain or enlighten us about it.

'But so long as Britain remained and held power, the differences would continue to exist. The Congress has made it clear that the future constitution will be framed not by the Congress alone but by the representatives of all political parties and religious groups. The Congress has gone further and declared that the minorities can have their representatives elected for this purpose by separate electorates though the Congress regards separate electorates as an evil. It will be representative of all the peoples of this country, irrespective of their religions and political affiliations, who will be deciding the future constitution of India and not this or that party. What better guarantee can the minorities have?' So according to Babu Rajendra Prasad, the moment we enter the Assembly we shall shed all our political affiliations and religions and everything else. This is what Babu Rajendra Prasad said as late as 18 March 1940. And this is now what Mr Gandhi said on 20 March 1940. He says: 'To me Hindus, Muslims, Parsees, Harijans, are all alike, I cannot be frivolous' but—I think he is frivolous—'I cannot be frivolous while I talk of Quaid-i-Azam Jinnah. He is my brother.'

The only difference is this, that brother Gandhi has three votes and I have only one vote!

'I would be happy indeed if he could keep me in his pockets.' I do not know really what to say to this latest offer of his. 'There was a time when I could say that there was no Muslim whose confidence I did not enjoy. It is my misfortune that it is not so today.'

Why has he lost the confidence of the Muslims today, may I ask, ladies and gentlemen?

'I do not read all that appears in the Urdu press, but perhaps I get a lot of abuse there. I am not sorry for it. I still believe that without Hindu-Muslim settlement there can be no Swaraj.'

Mr Gandhi has been saying this now for the last twenty years.

'You will perhaps ask in that case why do I talk of a fight? I do so because it is to be a fight for a Constituent Assembly.'

He is fighting the British. But may I point out to Mr Gandhi and the Congress that you are fighting for a Constituent Assembly which, the Muslims say, we cannot accept, which, the Muslims say, means three to one, about which the Musalmans say that they will never be able in that way, by the counting of heads, to come to any agreement which will be real agreement from the heart, which will enable us to work as friends and, therefore, this idea of a Constituent Assembly is objectionable, apart from other objections. But he is fighting for the Constituent Assembly, not fighting the Musalmans at all.

He says, 'I do so because it is to be a fight for a Constituent Assembly. If Muslims who come to the Constituent Assembly'— mark the words 'who come to the Constituent Assembly through Muslim votes': he is first forcing us to come to that Assembly—and then says, 'declare that there is nothing common between Hindus and Muslims then alone I would give up all hope, but even then I would agree with them because they read the Quran and I have also studied something of the Holy Book.'

So he wants the Constituent Assembly for the purpose of ascertaining the views of the Musalmans and if they do not agree then he will give up all hope, but even then he will agree with us? Well, I ask you, ladies and gentlemen, is this the way to show any real, genuine desire, if there existed any, to come to settlement with the Musalmans? Why does not Mr Gandhi agree, and I have suggested to him more than once and I repeat it again from this platform, why does not Mr Gandhi honestly now acknowledge that the Congress is a Hindu Congress, that he does not represent anybody except the solid body of Hindu people? Why should not Mr Gandhi be proud to say, 'I am a Hindu, Congress has solid Hindu backing'? I am not ashamed of saying that I am a Musalman. I am right and I hope and believe even a blind man must have been convinced by now that the Muslim League has the solid backing of the Musalmans of India. Why then all this camouflage? Why all these machinations? Why all these methods to coerce the British to overthrow the Musalmans? Why this declaration of non-cooperation? Why this threat of civil disobedience? And why fight for a Constituent Assembly for the sake of ascertaining whether the Musalmans agree or they do not agree? Why not come as a Hindu leader, proudly representing your people, and let me meet you, proudly representing the Musalmans? This is all that I have to say so far as the Congress is concerned.

So far as the British Government is concerned, our negotiations are not concluded yet, as you know. We had asked for assurances on several points, at any rate we have made some advance with regard to one point and that is this. You remember our demand was that the entire problem of the future constitution of India should be examined *de novo*, apart from the Government of India Act of 1935. To that the Viceroy's reply, with the authority of His Majesty's Government, was—I had better quote that—I will not put it in my own words. This is the reply that was sent to us on 23 December:

'My answer to your first question is that the declaration I made with the approval of His Majesty's Government on 13 October last does not exclude'—mark the words 'does not exclude'—'examination of any part either of the Act of 1935 or of the policy and plans on which it is based.'

As regards other matters, we are still negotiating and the most important points are that no declaration should be made by His Majesty's Government with regard to the future constitution of India without our approval and consent and that no settlement of any question should be made with any party behind our back unless our approval and consent is given to it. Well, ladies and gentlemen, whether the British Government in their wisdom agree to give us that assurance or not, I trust that they will still see that it is a fair and just demand when we say that we cannot leave the future fate and the destiny of 90 millions of people in the hands of any other judge. We and we alone wish to be the final arbiter. Surely that is a just demand. We do not want the British Government should thrust upon the Musalmans a constitution which they do not approve of and to which they do not agree. Therefore the British Government will be well advised to give that assurance and give the Musalmans complete peace and confidence in this matter and win their friendship. But whether they do that or not, after all, as I told you before, we must depend on our own inherent strength and I make it plain from this platform that if any declaration is made, if any interim settlement is made without our approval and without our consent, the Musalmans of India will resist. And no mistake should be made on that score.

Then the next point was with regard to Palestine. We are told that endeavours, earnest endeavours, are being made to meet the reasonable national demands of the Arabs. Well, we cannot be satisfied by earnest endeavours, sincere endeavours, best endeavours. We want that the British Government should in fact and actually meet the demands of the Arabs in Palestine.

Then the next point was with regard to the sending of the troops outside. Here there is some misunderstanding. But anyhow, we have made our position clear that we never intended, and, in fact, language does not justify it, if there is any misapprehension, or apprehension, that the Indian troops should not be used to the fullest in the defence of our own country. What we wanted the British Government to give us assurance of was that Indian troops should not be sent against any Muslim country or any Muslim power. Let us hope that we may yet be able to get the British Government to clarify the position further.

This, then, is the position with regard to the British Government. The last meeting of the Working Committee had asked the Viceroy to reconsider his letter of 23 December having regard to what has been explained to him in pursuance of the resolution of the Working Committee dated 3 February and we are informed that the matter is receiving his careful consideration. Ladies and gentlemen, that is where we stand after the war and up to 3 February.

As far as our internal position is concerned, we have also been examining it and, you know, there are several schemes which have been sent by various well-informed constitutionalists and others who take an interest in the problem of India's future constitution, and we have also appointed a sub-committee to examine the details of the schemes that have come in so far. But one thing is quite clear. It has always been taken for granted—mistakenly—that the Musalmans are a minority and of course we have got used to it for such a long time that these settled notions sometimes are very difficult to remove. The Musalmans are not a minority. The Musalmans are a nation by any definition. The British and particularly the Congress proceed on the basis, 'Well, you are a minority after all, what do you want? What else do the minorities want?' Just as Babu Rajendra Prasad said. But surely the Musalmans are not a minority. We find that even according to the British map of India, we occupy large parts of this country, where the Musalmans are in a majority—such as Bengal, Punjab, NWFP, Sindh, and Balochistan.

Now the question is, what is the best solution of this problem between the Hindus and the Musalmans? We have been considering, and as I have already said, a committee has been appointed to consider the various proposals. But whatever the final scheme of constitution I will present to you my views and I will just read to you in confirmation of what I am going to put before you a letter from Lala Lajpat Rai to Mr C.R. Das. It was written, I believe, about fourteen or fifteen years ago and that letter has been produced in a book by one Indira Prakash recently published and that is how this letter has come to light. This is what Lala Lajpat Rai, a very astute politician and a staunch Hindu Mahasabhite, said. But before I read this letter, it is plain from that you cannot get away from being a Hindu if you are Hindu! The word 'nationalist' has now become the play of conjurers in politics. This is what he says:

'There is one point more which has been troubling me very much of late and one which I want you to think carefully and that is the question of Hindu-Mohammedan unity. I have devoted most of my time during the last six months to the study of Muslim history and Muslim law and I am inclined to think it is neither possible nor practicable. Assuming and admitting the sincerity of

Mohammedan leaders in the non-cooperation movement, I think their religion provides an effective bar to anything of the kind.

'You remember the conversation I reported to you in Calcutta which I had with Hakim Ajmal Khan and Dr Kitchlu. There is no finer Mohammedan in Hindustan than Hakim Ajmal Khan, but can any Muslim leader override the Quran? I can only hope that my reading of the Islamic law is incorrect.'

I think his reading is quite correct.

'And nothing would relieve me more than to be convinced that it is so. But if it is right then it comes to this, that although we can unite against the British we cannot do so to rule Hindustan on British lines. We cannot do so to rule Hindustan *on democratic lines.*'

Ladies and gentlemen, when Lala Lajpat Rai said that we cannot rule this country on democratic lines, it was all right, but when I had the temerity to speak the same truth about eighteen months ago, there was a shower of attacks and criticism. But Lala Lajpat Rai said fifteen years ago that we cannot do so, viz., to rule Hindustan on democratic lines. What is the remedy? The remedy according to Congress is to keep us in the minority and under the majority rule. Lala Lajpat Rai proceeds further:

'What is then the remedy? I am not afraid of the seven crores of Musalmans. But I think the seven crores in Hindustan plus the armed hosts of Afghanistan, Central Asia, Arabia, Mesopotamia and Turkey will be irresistible.

'I do honestly and sincerely believe in the necessity or desirability of Hindu-Muslim unity. I am also fully prepared to trust the Muslim leaders. But what about the injunctions of the Quran and *hadith*? The leaders cannot override them. Are we then doomed? I hope your learned mind and wise head will find some way out of this difficulty.'

Now, ladies and gentlemen, that is merely a letter written by one great Hindu leader to another great Hindu leader fifteen years ago. Now, I should like to put before you my views on the subject as it strikes me, taking everything into consideration at the present moment. The British Government and Parliament, and more so the British nation, have been for many decades past brought up and nurtured with settled notions about India's future, based on developments in their own country which have built up the British constitution, functioning now through the Houses of Parliament and the system of Cabinet. Their concept of party government functioning on political planes has become the ideal with them as the best form of government for every country, and the one-sided and powerful propaganda, which naturally appeals to the British, has led them into a serious blunder, in producing the constitution envisaged in the Government of India Act of 1935. We find that most leading statesmen of Great Britain, saturated with these notions, have in their pronouncements seriously asserted and expressed a hope that the passage of time will harmonize the inconsistent elements in India.

A leading journal like the London *Times*, commenting on the Government of India Act of 1935, wrote, 'Undoubtedly the differences between the Hindus and Muslims are not of religion in the strict sense of the word but also of law and culture, that they may be said, indeed, to represent two entirely distinct and separate civilizations. However, in the course of time, the superstition will die out and India will be moulded into a single nation.' So, according to the London *Times*, the only difficulties are superstitions. These fundamental and deep-rooted differences, spiritual, economic, cultural, social, and political, have been euphemized as mere 'superstitions'. But surely it is a flagrant disregard of the past history of the subcontinent of India as well as the fundamental Islamic conception of society *vis-à-vis* that of Hinduism to characterize them as mere 'superstitions'. Notwithstanding 1,000 years of close contact, nationalities, which are as divergent today as ever, cannot at any time be expected to transform themselves into one nation merely by means of subjecting them to a democratic constitution and holding them forcibly together by unnatural and artificial methods of British Parliamentary Statute. What the unitary government of India for 150 years failed to achieve cannot be realized by the imposition of a Central Federal Government. It is inconceivable that the fiat or the writ of a government so constituted can ever command a willing and loyal obedience throughout the subcontinent by various nationalities except by means of armed force behind it.

The problem in India is not of an inter-communal character but manifestly of an international one, and it must be treated as such. So long as this basic and fundamental truth is not realized, any constitution that may be built will result in disaster and will prove destructive and harmful not only to the Musalmans but to the British and Hindus also. If the British Government are really in earnest and sincere to secure the peace and happiness of the people of this subcontinent, the only course open to us all is to allow the major nations separate homelands by dividing India into 'autonomous national States'. There is no reason why these States should be antagonistic to each other. On the other hand, the rivalry and the natural desire and efforts on the part of one to dominate the social order and establish political supremacy over the other in the government of the country will disappear. It will lead more towards natural goodwill by international pacts between them, and they can live in complete harmony with their neighbours. This will lead further to a friendly settlement all the more easily with regard to minorities by reciprocal arrangements and adjustments between Muslim India and Hindu India, which will far more adequately and effectively safeguard the rights and interests of Muslims and various other minorities.

It is extremely difficult to appreciate why our Hindu friends fail to understand the real nature of Islam and Hinduism. They are not religions in the strict sense of the word, but are, in fact, different and distinct social orders, and it is a dream that the Hindus and Muslims can ever evolve a common nationality, and this misconception of one Indian nation has gone far beyond the limits and is the cause of most of your troubles and will lead India to destruction if we fail to revise our notions in time. The Hindus and Muslims belong to two different religious philosophies, social customs, literature. They neither intermarry nor dine together and, indeed, they belong to two different civilizations which are based mainly on conflicting ideas and conceptions. Their aspects on life and of life are different. It is quite clear that Hindus and Musalmans derive their inspiration from different sources of history. They have different epics, different heroes, and different episodes. Very often the hero of one is a foe of the other and, likewise, their victories and defeats overlap. To yoke together two such nations under a single State, one as a numerical minority and the other as a majority, must lead to growing discontent and final destruction of any fabric that may be so built up for the government of such a State.

History has presented to us many examples, such as the Union of Great Britain and Ireland, Czechoslovakia and Poland. History has also shown to us many geographical tracts, much smaller than the subcontinent of India, which otherwise might have been called one country, but which have been divided into as many States as there are nations inhabiting them. The Balkan Peninsula comprises as many as seven or eight sovereign States. Likewise, the Portuguese and the Spanish stand divided in the Iberian Peninsula. Whereas under the plea of unity of India and one nation, which does not exist, it is sought to pursue here the line of one central government when we know that the history of the last 1,200 years has failed to achieve unity and has witnessed, during the ages, India always divided into Hindu India and Muslim India. The present artificial unity of India dates back only to the British conquest and is maintained by the British bayonet, but termination of the British regime, which is implicit in the recent declaration of His Majesty's Government, will be the herald of the entire break-up with worse disaster than has ever taken place during the last 1,000 years under Muslims. Surely that is not the legacy which Britain would bequeath to India after 150 years of her rule, nor would Hindu and Muslim India risk such a sure catastrophe.

Muslim India cannot accept any constitution which must necessarily result in a Hindu majority government. Hindus and Muslims brought together under a democratic system forced upon the minorities can only mean Hindu Raj. Democracy of the kind with which the Congress High Command is enamoured would mean the complete destruction of what is most precious in Islam.

We have had ample experience of the working of the provincial constitutions during the last two and a half years and any repetition of such a government must lead to civil war and raising of private armies as recommended by Mr Gandhi to Hindus of Sukkur when he said that they must defend themselves violently or non-violently, blow for blow, and if they could not, they must emigrate.

Musalmans are not a minority as it is commonly known and understood. One has only got to look around. Even today, according to the British map of India, four out of eleven provinces, where the Muslims dominate more or less, are functioning notwithstanding the decision of the Hindu Congress High Command to non-cooperate and prepare for civil disobedience. Musalmans are a nation according to any definition of a nation, and they must have their homelands, their territory, and their State. We wish to live in peace and harmony with our neighbours as a free and independent people. We wish our people to develop to the fullest our spiritual, cultural, economic, social, and political life in a way that we think best and in consonance with our own ideals and according to the genius of our people. Honesty demands and the vital interests of millions of our people impose a sacred duty upon us to find an honourable and peaceful solution, which would be just and fair to all. But at the same time we cannot be moved or diverted from our purpose and objective by threats or intimidations. We must be prepared to face all difficulties and consequences, make all the sacrifices that may be required of us to achieve the goal we have set in front of us.

Ladies and gentlemen, I have placed before you the task that lies ahead of us. Do you realize how big and stupendous it is? Do you realize that you cannot get freedom or independence by mere arguments? I should appeal to the intelligentsia. The intelligentsia in all countries in the world have been the pioneers of any movements for freedom. What does the Muslim intelligentsia propose to do? I may tell you that unless you get this into your blood, unless you are prepared to take off your coats and are willing to sacrifice all that you can and work selflessly, earnestly, and sincerely for your people, you will never realize your aim. Friends,

I therefore want you to make up your mind definitely and then think of devices and organize your people, strengthen your organization and consolidate the Musalmans all over India. I think that the masses are wide awake. They only want your guidance and your lead. Come forward as servants of Islam, organize the people economically, socially, educationally, and politically and I am sure that you will be a power that will be accepted by everybody.

Dr Sir Mohammad Iqbal of Lincoln's Inn Barrister and the poet philosopher who, in his presidential address to the All-India Muslim League session at Allahabad in 1930, first suggested a separate homeland for Muslims in the Muslim majority provinces of India. [Ed.]

The name Pakistan was coined in 1933 by a Cambridge-based scholar, Chaudhry Rehmat Ali, and was later adopted by the Muslim League for the proposed Muslim State after the Lahore session of 22–24 March 1940, when the historic Lahore Resolution was passed demanding a separate homeland for Muslims in Muslim majority provinces in India. For the text of the resolution passed see *Chronology*. [Ed.]

20

COMMENT ON THE SPEECH

He spoke for nearly two hours, his voice now deep and trenchant, now light and ironic. Such was the dominance of his personality that despite the improbability of more than a fraction of his audience [100,000] understanding English, he held his hearers and played with palpable effect on their emotions.

The Times of India.

21

THE TASK AHEAD

Extract from the Quaid-i-Azam's Presidential Address to the
Constituent Assembly of Pakistan, 11 August 1947*

I cordially thank you, with the utmost sincerity, for the honour you have conferred upon me—the greatest honour that is possible for this Sovereign Assembly to confer—by electing me as your first president. I also thank those leaders who spoke in appreciation of my services and their personal references to me. I sincerely hope that with your support and your co-operation we shall make this Constituent Assembly an example to the world. The Constituent Assembly has got two main functions to perform. The first is the very onerous and responsible task of framing our future constitution of Pakistan and the second of functioning as a full and complete sovereign body as the Federal Legislature of Pakistan. We have to do the best we can in adopting a provisional Constitution for the Federal Legislature of Pakistan. You know really that not only we ourselves are wondering but, I think, the whole world is wondering at this unprecedented cyclonic revolution which has

---

*Constituent Assembly of Pakistan was formed on 11 August 1947 two days before the declaration of independence: 14 August 1947.

brought about the plan of creating and establishing two independent sovereign dominions in this subcontinent. As it is, it has been unprecedented; there is no parallel in the history of the world. This mighty subcontinent with all kinds of inhabitants has been brought under a plan which is titanic, unknown, unparalleled. And what is very important with regard to it is that we have achieved it peacefully and by means of an evolution of the greatest possible character.

Dealing with our first function in this Assembly, I cannot make any well-considered pronouncement at this moment, but I shall say a few things as they occur to me. The first and the foremost thing that I would like to emphasize is this—remember that you are now a sovereign legislative body and you have got all the powers. It, therefore, places on you the gravest responsibility as to how you should take your decisions. The first observation that I would like to make is this: you will no doubt agree with me that the first duty of a government is to maintain law and order, so that the life, property, and religious beliefs of its subjects are fully protected by the state.

I know there are people who do not quite agree with the division of India and the partition of the Punjab and Bengal. Much has been said against it, but now that it has been accepted, it is the duty of every one of us to loyally abide by it and honourably act according to the agreement which is now final and binding on all. But you must remember, as I have said, that this mighty revolution that has taken place is unprecedented. One can quite understand the feeling that exists between the two communities wherever one community is in majority and the other is in minority. But the question is whether it was possible or practicable to act otherwise than has been done. A division had to take place. On both sides, in Hindustan and Pakistan, there are sections of people who may not agree with it, who may not like it, but in my judgement there was no other solution and I am sure future history will record its verdict in favour of it. And, what is more, it will be proved by actual experience as we go on that it was the only solution to India's constitutional problem. Any idea of a United India could have led us to terrific disaster. Maybe that view is correct; maybe it is not; that remains to be seen. All the same, in this division it was impossible to avoid the question of minorities being in one Dominion or the other. Now that was unavoidable. There is no other solution. Now what shall we do? Now, if we want to make this great State of Pakistan happy and prosperous we should wholly and solely concentrate on the well-being of the people, and especially of the masses and the poor. If you will work in co-operation, forgetting the past, burying the hatchet, you are bound to succeed. If you change your past and work together in a spirit that everyone of you, no matter to what community he belongs, no matter what relations he had with you in the past, no matter what is his colour, caste, or creed, is first, second, and last a citizen of this State with equal rights, privileges, and obligations, there will be no end to the progress you will make.

I cannot emphasize it too much. We should begin to work in that spirit and in course of time all these angularities of the majority and minority communities, the Hindu community and the Muslim community—because even as regards Muslims you have Pathans, Punjabis, Shias, Sunnis, and so on and among the Hindus you have Brahmins, Vashnvas, Khatris, also Bengalis, Madrasis, and so on—will vanish. Indeed, if you ask me, this has been the biggest hindrance in the way of India to attain the freedom and independence and, but for this, we would have been free people long, long ago. No power can hold another nation, and specially a nation of 400 million souls, in subjection; nobody could have conquered you, and even if it had happened, nobody could have continued its hold on you for any length of time but for this. Therefore we must learn a lesson from this. You are free; you are free to go to your temples, you are free to go to your mosques or to any other places of worship in this State of Pakistan. You may belong to any religion or caste or creed—that has nothing to do with the business of the State. As you know, history shows that in England conditions some time ago were much worse than those prevailing in India today. The Roman Catholics and the Protestants persecuted each other. Even now there are some States in existence where there are discriminations made and bars imposed against a particular class. Thank God we are not starting in those days. We are starting in the days when there is no discrimination, no distinction between one community and another, no discrimination between one caste or creed and another. We are starting with this fundamental principle that we are all citizens and equal citizens of one State. The people of England in course of time had to face the realities of the situation and had to discharge the responsibilities and burdens placed upon them by the government of their country and they went through that fire step by step. Today you might say with justice that Roman Catholics and Protestants do not exist; what exists now is that every man is a citizen, and equal citizen, of Great Britain and they are all members of the nation.

Now, I think we should keep that in front of us as our ideal and you will find that in course of time Hindus would cease to be Hindus and Muslims would cease to be Muslims, not in the religious sense, because that is the personal faith of each individual, but in the political sense as citizens of the State.

Well, gentlemen, I do not wish to take up any more of your time and thank you again for the honour you have done to me. I shall always be guided by the principles of justice and fair play without any, as is put in the political language, prejudice or ill-will, in other words, partiality or favouritism. My guiding principle will be justice and complete impartiality, and I am sure that with your support and co-operation, I can look forward to Pakistan becoming one of the greatest nations of the world.

22

EXTRACTS FROM
VARIOUS SPEECHES*

Real Mother

Mr Rajagopalacharya's arguments of dividing the baby and the parable of King Solomon have gone beyond the zenith of his intellectual powers. This analogy he wants to apply to our proposals. Surely, India is not the sole property of the Congress and if the real mother was to be discovered it would be the Dravidians and still further the aborigines. It would neither be the Aryan nor the Musalman. The Aryan claim to India is no better than that of the Musalmans except that they were earlier arrivals in point of time.

Liquidation of the British Empire

You know, Mr Churchill, some time ago, said that he was not called or summoned to be the first Minister of the King to preside over the liquidation of the British Empire. Now I can tell him this, that voluntary liquidation is more honourable than a compulsory one.

* Some recent speeches and writings of Mr Jinnah, collected and edited by Jamil-ud-Din Ahmed (Lahore: Sheikh Muhammad Ashraf [4th ed. 1946]), p. 186.

It will redound to the honour of the British nation, and it will be recognized by us as an act of friendship which has got its value and assets in the future. But compulsory liquidation will have none of those advantages, and the British Empire will have to be liquidated one day, whether you like it or not.

Presidential speech at the session of the All-India Muslim League, Karachi, 24 December 1943.

MUSLIM WOMEN

I am glad to see that not only Muslim men but Muslim women and children also have understood the Pakistan scheme. No nation can make any progress without the co-operation of its women. If Muslim women support their men, as they did in the days of the Prophet of Islam, we should soon realize our goal.

Speech at Jinnah Islamia College for Girls, Lahore, 22 November 1942.

MAJORITY RULE

Democracy means, to begin with, majority rule. Majority rule in a single nation, in a single society is understandable...Representative government in a single nation, harmonious, homogeneous, and one is understandable. But you have only got to apply your mind for a few minutes to see the truth. Can such a system ever work or succeed when you have two different nations—indeed more than two different nations—in this subcontinent, when you have two totally different societies, the Muslim Society and the Hindu Society?

Presidential address at the session of the All-India Muslim League, Madras, April 1941.

DEMOCRACY AND ARMED FORCES

You have fought many a battle on the farflung battlefields of the globe to rid the world of the Fascist menace and make it safe for democracy. Now you have to stand guard over the development and maintenance of Islamic democracy, Islamic social justice, and the equality of manhood, in your own native soil.

Address to Anti-Aircraft Regiments in Malir, 2 February 1948.

35 Russell Road, Kensington, London, where Jinnah stayed in 1895

JINNAH
AND
ISLAMIC BANKING

23

JINNAH'S ADDRESS TO THE STATE BANK OF PAKISTAN

Speech on the occasion of the opening ceremony of
State Bank of Pakistan, Karachi, 1 July 1948

'Mr Governor, Directors of the State Bank, Ladies and Gentlemen!

'The opening of the State Bank of Pakistan symbolizes the sovereignty of our State in the financial sphere and I am very glad to be here today to perform the opening ceremony. It was not considered feasible to start a Bank of our own simultaneously with the coming into being of Pakistan in August last year. A good deal of preparatory work must precede the inauguration of an institution responsible for such technical and delicate work as note issue and banking. To allow for this preparation, it was provided, under the Pakistan Monetary System and Reserve Bank Order, 1947, that the Reserve Bank of India should continue to be the currency and banking authority in Pakistan till the 30 September 1948. Later on it was felt that it would be in the best interests of our State if the Reserve Bank of India were relieved of its functions in Pakistan as early as possible. The date of transfer of these functions to a

Pakistan agency was consequently advanced by three months in agreement with the Government of India and the Reserve Bank. It was at the same time decided to establish a Central Bank of Pakistan in preference to any other agency for managing our currency and banking. This decision left very little time for the small band of trained personnel in this field in Pakistan to complete the preliminaries and they have by their untiring effort and hard work completed their task by the due date which is very creditable to them, and I wish to record a note of our appreciation of their labours.

'As you have observed, Mr Governor, in undivided India banking was kept a close preserve of non-Muslims and their migration from Western Pakistan has caused a good deal of dislocation in the economic life of our young State. In order that the wheels of commerce and industry should run smoothly, it is imperative that the vacuum caused by the exodus of non-Muslims should be filled without delay. I am glad to note that schemes for training Pakistan nationals in banking are in hand. I will watch their progress with interest and I am confident that the State Bank will receive the co-operation of all concerned including the banks and universities in pushing them forward. Banking will provide a new and wide field in which the genius of our young men can find full play. I am sure that they will come forward in large numbers to take advantage of the training facilities which are proposed to be provided. While doing so, they will not only be benefiting themselves but also contributing to the well-being of our State.

'I need hardly dilate on the important role that the State Bank will have to play in regulating the economic life of our country. The monetary policy of the bank will have a direct bearing on our trade and commerce, both inside Pakistan as well as with the outside world and it is only to be desired that your policy should encourage maximum production and a free flow of trade. The monetary policy pursued during the war years contributed, in no small measure, to our present day economic problems. The abnormal rise in the cost of living has hit the poorer sections of society including those with fixed incomes very hard indeed and is responsible to a great extent for the prevailing unrest in the country. The policy of the Pakistan Government is to stabilize prices at a level that would be fair to the producer, as well as to the consumer. I hope your efforts will be directed in the same direction in order to tackle this crucial problem with success.

'I shall watch with keenness the work of your Research Organization in evolving practices compatible with Islamic ideals of social and economic life. The economic system of the West has created almost insoluble problems for humanity and to many of us it appears that only a miracle can save it from disaster that is now facing the world. It has failed to do justice between man and man and to eradicate friction form the international field. On the contrary it was largely responsible for the two world wars in the last half century. The Western world, in spite of its advantages of mechanization and industrial efficiency is today in a worse mess than ever before in history. The adoption of Western economic theory and practice will not help us in achieving our goal of creating a happy and contented people. We must work our destiny in our own way and present to the world an economic system based on true Islamic concept of equality of manhood and social justice. We will thereby be fulfilling our mission as Muslims and giving to humanity the message of peace which alone can save it and secure the welfare, happiness and prosperity of mankind.

'May the State Bank of Pakistan prosper and fulfill the high ideals which have been set as its goal!

'In the end I thank you, Mr Governor, for the warm welcome given to me by you and your colleagues and the distinguished guests who have graced this occasion as a mark of their good wishes and the honour you have done me in inviting me to perform this historic opening ceremony of the State Bank which I feel will develop into one of our greatest national institutions and play its part fully throughout the world.' (A.P.I.)

(The Civil & Military Gazette, 2 July 1948)

24

ISLAMIC FINANCE AND BANKING
Philip Molyneux

INTRODUCTION

In his address at the opening ceremony of the State Bank of Pakistan on 1 July 1948, the founder of the country stated that it would be in the interests of the economy to consider an economic and financial system based on Islamic principles, particularly as Western economic thought had brought about a spectacularly unsuccessful framework for advancements in the world he knew. Little would Jinnah have expected that, over 60 years later, Islamic banking and finance principles would be the talk of Western economists, bankers, and policymakers, as a model on which to guide the re-introduction of ethical principles into the collapsed Western financial systems! He would also probably be astonished to know that by 2008 Shariah-compliant banks held assets amounting to nearly $700 billion; Islamic banking and finance activities cover the globe, with all major global commercial banks having their own Islamic subsidiaries; and investment banks are arranging and issuing *Sukuk* bonds and other Shariah-compliant investment services.

Islamic banking that started on a modest scale in the 1960s has shown exceptional growth. What started as a small rural banking experiment in the remote villages of Egypt has now reached a level where many international banks now offer Islamic banking and financial products. Islamic banking has spread from the East to the West, all the way from Indonesia and Malaysia to Europe and the Americas. Forty years ago, Islamic banking was considered to be not much more than wishful thinking but now it is a reality. It has been shown to be both feasible and viable, and can operate just as efficiently and productively as Western-style financial intermediation. The successful operation of these institutions and their experiences in Pakistan, Iran, Malaysia, Saudi Arabia, Bahrain, and throughout the Islamic world demonstrate that the alternative suggested by Jinnah offers both a viable and successful alternative to Western commercial banking and finance. The fact that many conventional banks are also using Islamic banking and finance techniques is further proof of the viability of the Islamic alternative. Even though Islamic banks emerged in response to the needs of their Muslim clients, they are not religious institutions. Like any other type of bank, they are profit-seeking institutions. (Jinnah may have been pleased to learn that one of the most profitable banks in the world, and the most profitable Islamic bank, in 2007 was Habib Bank— a conventional Pakistani bank with an Islamic division!) Islamic banks use a different model of financial intermediation, and it is the features of this model that have attracted the attention of international financiers and policy makers. There has been a new dynamism in recent years as this industry has proved increasingly attractive, not only to the world's 1.6 billion Muslims, but also to many others who are beginning to understand the unique aspects of Islamic banking and finance.

KEY PRINCIPLES OF ISLAMIC FINANCE

The main (and most well known) principle of Islamic finance is the prohibition of interest (*Riba*). This means that financial contracts and other activities have to be constructed in a way that omits the receipt or payment of interest. Probably the second best-known principle is the prohibition of gambling and other activities forbidden under Islamic law—this means that banks cannot make loans to casinos, alcohol producers, and so on. Islamic investment funds, for instance, have Shariah boards that screen out investments in non-Islamic compliant businesses. A final main principle, the prohibition of *Gharar*, is lesser known and more complex. This refers to acts and conditions in exchange contracts, the full implications of which are not clearly known to the parties. It is similar to what we refer to as 'asymmetric information'—differences in information between contracting parties. Where these are large, and there is the opportunity for one party to take material advantage of their position, then the contract is regarded as anti-Islamic. Islamic jurisprudence relies on the general condition of trustworthiness of the contracting parties to deal with this. With regard to the aforementioned three main principles, all Islamic financial firms have Shariah boards that oversee activities, to ensure that their operations comply with Islamic principles.

The function of financial intermediation requires the provision of mechanisms for saving and borrowing, so that agents in the economy can alleviate budget constraints. This involves creating a variety of financial assets and liabilities with different characteristics that appeal to different savers and borrowers. Conventional commercial banks provide financial intermediation services on the basis of rates of interest (charged and paid) on both the assets' and the liabilities' side. Since interest is prohibited in Islam, Islamic banks have developed various other modes through which savings are mobilized and passed on to entrepreneurs, none of which involve interest. Similarly, for the provision of other financial services, such as payment services, insurance, fund management, etc., Islamic banks have developed alternative contracts which are compatible with Shariah law. Overall, the core tenets of Islamic finance relate to: a ban on charging interest, a commitment to profit-and-loss sharing (in place of interest-based transactions), and asset-backed transactions.

While the types of Islamic banking products and services can vary from country-to-country, if we look at Pakistan as an example, the main lending products offered by the banks are as follows:

Murabaha (sales contract) This relates to various trading contracts, where the sale of goods is specified at a set profit margin. Here, the bank purchases the goods desired by the borrower (e.g., a car) which the bank then sells on at an agreed marked-up price. Payment is settled within an agreed time frame, either in instalments or in a lump sum. The bank bears the risk for the goods until they have been delivered to the buyer (borrower).

Diminishing *Musharakah* This is a profit and loss sharing partnership contract of a particular form. A traditional *Musharakah* contract involves both the partners to the contract (the bank and borrower) participating in the management and provision of the capital, and sharing in the profit and loss of the project for which the funds have been lent. Profits are distributed between the partners according to the ratios set at the onset of the contract, whereas losses are distributed according to proportion based on each partner's share in the capital. Diminishing *Musharakah* has evolved from the former, and involves the bank and client participating in either joint ownership of property or equipment, or in a joint commercial enterprise. The share of the bank is further divided into a number of units. It is understood that the client will periodically purchase the units of the bank's share, one at a time, so increasing the client's share until all the units of the bank have been purchased—when the client becomes the sole owner of the property or commercial enterprise, as the case may be. Diminishing *Musharakah* can assume different forms in the various transactions; traditionally, it has mainly been used in housing finance.

Ijarah These are generally viewed as leasing agreements. Under this concept, banks make the use of various assets/equipment (such as a plant, office equipment, cars) available to clients for a fixed period and price.

Salam (Purchase by order) *Salam* is a sale whereby the bank undertakes to supply specific goods to the buyer at a future date in exchange for an advanced price that has been paid in full on the spot.

Istisna This is similar to *Salam* but involves a sale in which a commodity is transacted before it comes into existence. For instance, it may involve the financing of the purchase of manufactured goods before they have been fabricated. The price is fixed with the consent of the parties, as is the specification of the commodity to be manufactured. The difference between *Istisna* and *Salam* is that, in the former, goods that need to be manufactured are always involved, whereas *Salam* contracts can cover any item. Also, in *Salam* contracts the price has to be paid in advance, while this is not necessary in *Istisna*.

Querd-e-Hasnah These are loans that are given on compassionate grounds, free of any charges and repayable if and when the borrower is able to repay them.

According to the State Bank of Pakistan (December 2007), in terms of the types of financing, *Murabaha* was used for almost 45 per cent of total Islamic banking financing, followed by Diminishing *Musharakah* (25 per cent) and *Ijarah* (24 per cent). Other types of contracts—*Salam*, *Istisna*, and *Querd-e-Hasnah*—account for the remaining 6 per cent.

ISLAMIC BANKING IN PAKISTAN

While Jinnah's request to the Pakistani monetary authorities to adopt an alternative to Western style finance and economic management was made in 1948, the process of economy-wide Islamisation of the country's banking system was not initiated until 1979. In February of that year, the government announced plans to rid the economy of interest within a period of three years, and that a decision had been taken to make a beginning in this direction with the elimination of interest payment from various specialist financing firms—the House Building Finance Corporation, National Investment Trust, and mutual funds of the Investment Corporation of Pakistan. Soon after this, these specialized financial institutions took various steps to adapt their activities to non-interest based ones.

The conversion of the country's commercial banks to Islamic institutions was somewhat more convoluted. In January 1981, separate counters were established to accept deposits on a profit/loss sharing basis in all domestic branches of the main nationalized commercial banks; this system existed up until mid-1985. From July, no banking company was permitted to take interest-bearing domestic currency deposits (although foreign currency deposits could still earn interest). As of that day, all deposits accepted by the banks were shared in its profit and loss, with the exception of deposits in the current accounts—no interest or profit was given, and the capital sum was guaranteed.

Over the following twenty years or so, there was ongoing debate between the monetary authorities, Islamic scholars, and the banks about the appropriate modes of Islamic structures, and the oversight of Islamic banks in general. Typically, arguments were mainly focused on which types of financing arrangements were or were not Islamic-compliant. By 2004, some form of general consensus emerged; the government continues to promote a mixed system, whereby conventional and Islamic banking compete side by side. All commercial banks are allowed to set-up Islamic windows and licenses are granted on a case-by-case basis.

By 2007, out of a total of 46 banks operating in the country, six were fully fledged Islamic banks: AIB Albaraka Islamic Bank B.S.C. (E.C.) (with 12 branches); BIP Bank Islamic Pakistan Limited (14 branches); DIB Dubai Islamic Bank Pakistan Ltd (17 branches); DWD Dawood Islamic Bank Limited (1 branch); EGI Emirates Global Islamic Bank Ltd (6 branches); and MBL Meezan Bank Limited (72 branches). As its substantial number of branches suggests, MBL Meezan Bank is by far the largest, accounting for 37 per cent of Islamic banking deposits and 34 per cent of assets.

In addition, 12 conventional banks had Islamic banking divisions or windows (separate counters) operating within 103 branches. The Islamic banking network has increased rapidly—the total number of branches increased from only 150 in 2006 to 288 in 2007, covering 25 cities and towns in all four provinces of the country.

Despite the number of Islamic banks operating in the country, their domestic market share is small. They account for only a little over 4 per cent of the total banking sector's deposits and assets. Table 1 illustrates that, in value terms, they lend mainly to the consumer and corporate sector; however, in terms of their total share of borrowers, this is under one percent!

Table 1: Islamic Banking Sector Market Shares

Sector	Banking Industry of Pakistan		Islamic Banking (IB) Industry of Pakistan		Mkt. Share of IB (Percentage)	
	No. of Borrowers	Amount (Rs. Mln.)	No. of Borrowers	Amount (Rs. Mln.)	No. of Borrowers	Amount (Rs. Mln.)
Corporate	26,061	1,520,130	1,959	62,784	7.5%	4.1%
SME Sector	185,039	437,351	2,685	12,535	1.5%	2.9%
Agriculture	1,415,353	150,777	159	13	0.0%	0.0%
Consumer Sector (other than staff loans)	3,025,463	371,421	36,533	28,843	1.2%	7.8%
Commodity Financing	2,616	148,447	31	1,118	1.2%	0.8%
Others	126,021	72,758	1,148	2,459	0.9%	3.3%
Total	4,780,553	2,700,884	42,515	107,752	0.9%	4.0%

Source: Islamic Banking Sector Review 2003 to 2007, State Bank of Pakistan (December 2007), p. 37.

THE FUTURE OF ISLAMIC BANKING IN PAKISTAN

Jinnah's desire to provide the now 160 million Pakistani populous with an economic and financial system based on Islamic principles has started from a low base but is gradually gaining credence. The 97 per cent Muslim population offers substantial opportunities for Islamic banking to penetrate deeper into the financial transactions of the economy. In a bold attempt to bolster the sector, the central bank has developed a strategy that aims to increase Islamic banking's market share to 12 per cent (from its current 4 per cent level). This is coupled with plans to improve regulation and strengthen Shariah compliance throughout the banking sector. Areas particularly targeted are the micro finance, agriculture, and small business lending sectors—areas that Islamic banks have typically found difficult to penetrate given the limited product set available. The aim is to encourage banks to roll-out new Islamic compliant products to target these areas. The central bank has engaged in benchmarking exercises, comparing products available in other Islamic banking countries, and aims to encourage the adoption of best-practice services in the domestic market. It is also likely to encourage the provision of Islamic credit cards and insurance products as well. Overall, the sector is expected to grow rapidly over the next few years.

CONCLUSION

Jinnah's call for a new financial and economic paradigm to complement Western economic philosophy and capitalist ideas has certainly become a reality but it still has a long way to develop, even in his own country, if it is to surpass the importance of interest-based banking on the global stage. Despite their rapid growth in recent years, the assets' size of the top 500 Islamic banks (in 2007) amounted to only 0.7 per cent of the total assets of the top 500 Western banks! However, the key features of Islamic banking—no interest being charged, profit-and-loss sharing contracts, and the emphasis on asset-backed transactions—have meant that Islamic banks have shied away from the complicated securitized asset business that has led to the collapse of Western institutions. (The most recent estimates suggest that, by July 2009, the US government had dedicated around $3 trillion of taxpayers' funds to bailout its banking system). Islamic banks, whose profits have remained strong, have relied on plentiful Muslim depositors, rather than the international debt markets, to finance their growth. Confidence in the reigning secular financial architecture has also been severely shaken, and an increasing number of commentators are looking at the success of Islamic banking to see if lessons can be learnt in formulating a new and safer operational and regulatory structure for Western banks.

While the short-term policy response to the Western financial crisis—injecting massive amounts of capital and liquidity into the US, UK, and other systems—appears to have been effective (so far) in minimizing the likelihood of a deflationary spiral, there is still an extensive policy debate surrounding the longer-term implications of the crisis—for the future architecture of the banking and financial system. When Jinnah gave his speech at the opening ceremony of the State Bank of Pakistan, he noted that 'The Western world, in spite of its advantages of mechanization and industrial efficiency, is today in a worse mess than ever before in history.' The same can perhaps be said of today, given the impact of the credit crunch and collapse of Western financial systems. What will emerge is a new economic environment and financial structure, informed by both Western and Islamic ideas, that seeks to establish a safer and more equitable financial system—founded more (as Jinnah would have wanted) on the principles of social justice and fairness to society rather than on the capitalist principles of avarice and greed.

Bibliography

Akhtar, S. (2007), 'Islamic Banking: Past, Present and Future Outlook', Keynote address by the Governor of the State Bank of Pakistan, at Dawn Asia Finance Conference, Karachi, 11 September 2007, http://www.bis.org/review/r070928e.pdf.

Hassan, M. (2007), 'The Islamization of the Economy and the Development of Islamic Banking in Pakistan', Kyoto Bulletin of Islamic Area Studies, 1–2, 92–109.

Iqbal, M. and Molyneux, P. (2005), *Thirty Years of Islamic Banking*, Palgrave Macmillan, London.

State Bank of Pakistan (2008), 'Strategic Plan for Islamic Banking', Islamic Banking Department of the State Bank of Pakistan.

Philip Molyneux is currently Professor in Banking and Finance and Head of Bangor Business School at Bangor University. He has published widely in the banking and financial services area, including articles in European Economic Review, Journal of Banking and Finance, Journal of Money, Credit and Banking, Economics Letters, and Economica. In 2001, he was the Visiting Bertill Daniellson Research Fellow at the Stockholm School of Economics and University of Gothenburg. Between 2002 and 2005, he has acted as a member of the ECON Financial Services expert panel for the European Parliament. His most recent co-authored texts are on: *Thirty Years of Islamic Banking* (Palgrave Macmillan, 2005), *Shareholder Value in Banking* (Palgrave Macmillan, 2006), and *Introduction to Banking* (FT Prentice Hall, 2006). He is currently co-editing (with Berger and Wilson) the *Oxford Handbook of Banking*. His main research interests focus on the structural features of banking systems, modelling bank performance, Islamic banking, and wealth management. He has recently held visiting professorships at Bocconi University, Erasmus University, and Bolzano Free University (Italy), where he taught MBA and other postgraduate students courses on private banking in Europe, research topics in banking, and various financial institution seminars. He has acted as a consultant to: New York Federal Reserve Bank, World Bank, European Commission, UK Treasury, Citibank Private Bank, Bermuda Commercial Bank, McKinsey's, Credit Suisse, and various other international banks and consulting firms.

25

CHRONOLOGY
QUAID-I-AZAM MOHAMMAD ALI JINNAH, 1876–1948
Salim Al-Din Quraishi

1876*: 25 December	Mahomedalli Jinnahbhai born in Newham Road, Karachi. Mother: Shirin Bai, also called Mithi Bai. Father Jinnahbhai Poonja.
1883–886	Studied at Sindh Madrasatul-Islam, Karachi.
1886	Moved to Bombay. Joined Gokal Das Tej Primary School.
1891: 5 January	Joined Christian Missionary Society High School, Karachi.
1892: February	Left Karachi for Paneli, Gondal State, Kathiawar, to marry Miss Emibai, daughter of an Ismaili wood merchant, Leera Khemji. Miss Emibai died shortly after Jinnah reached England.
1892: November	Left for England. Joined Grahams Shipping and Trading Company, London. Later, decided to enrol for the Bar at Lincoln's Inn. Stayed at 40 Glazbury Road, West Kensington, London.

* As recognized officially in Pakistan.

1893: February	Moved to 35 Russell Road, Kensington, London.
1893: 25 April	Applied for exemption from the Latin portion of the Preliminary Examination of Lincoln's Inn. Granted.
1893: 25 May	Awarded certificate of having passed the Preliminary Examination of Lincoln's Inn.
1893: 5 June	Admitted to Lincoln's Inn.
1893: September	Jinnah's mother died.
1895: 7 January	Applied to join the British Museum (now the British Library) as a reader, 'for references generally and specially to some oriental works.'
1895: 30 March	Applies to Lincoln's Inn Council to have his name altered on the Books of the Society from Mahomedalli Jinnahbhai to Mahomed Alli Jinnah.
1895: 14 April	Petition to have his name altered granted.
1896: 29 April	Called to the Bar.
1896: 11 May	Applied to Lincoln's Inn Council for a certificate of his admission call to the Bar and of his deportment.
1896: May	Returned to Karachi. Started legal practice at Karachi Bar Council.
1897–	Moved to Bombay. Enrolled as advocate at Bombay High Court.
1900: 3 May	Presidency Magistrate, Bombay.
1902	Started his political career.
1902: 17 April	Jinnah's father, Jinnah Poonja, died in Bombay.
1903: September	Appointed legal adviser, Municipal Corporation, Bombay.
1905: September	Left for London as member of Congress Delegation to plead for Indian self-government.

1906: March	Resigned from membership of the Bombay Corporation.
1906: 26–29 December	Attended the Calcutta Session of the Indian National Congress and acted as Private Secretary to Dadabhai Naoroji, President, Indian National Congress, Calcutta Session.
1906: 30 December	Foundation of All-India Muslim League at Dhaka Session of the Mohammedan Educational Conference.
1907: 8 January	Elected Vice-President, Indian Musalman Association, Calcutta.
1908: December	Elected Member, All-India Congress Committee at Congress Session, Madras.
1910: 4 January	Elected to Imperial Legislative Council by non-official members.
1910: February	Invited to address Muslim League Council meeting.
1910: 29 December	Attended Annual Session of All-India Congress at Allahabad.
1911: 1 January	Participated in Hindu-Muslim unity conference, Allahabad, under the Chairmanship of Sir William Wedderburn.
1912: 28–29 December	Attended All-India Muslim Educational Conference at Lucknow.
1912: 31 December	Attended Muslim League Council meeting at Bankipur, Bihar, under the Chairmanship of the Aga Khan.
1913: 11 January	Nominated Additional Member of the Imperial Legislative Council by the Viceroy, to enable him to introduce the Waqf Validating Bill.
1913: 22–23 March	Attended Lucknow Session of All-India Muslim League as a guest.
1913: April	Came to England with Gokhale.

1913: May	Founded London Indian Association.
1913: 28 June	Addressed public meeting of Indian students at Caxton Hall.
1913: 14 July	Attended Fifth Annual Meeting of London Muslim League under the Presidency of the Aga Khan who enlisted his support to improve relations between various communities in India.
1913: October	While in London, Maulana Muhammad Ali Jauhar formally enrolled him as a member of the All-India Muslim League; returned to India with Gokhale.
1913: 30–31 December	Attended Agra Session of All-India Muslim League for the first time as an official member.
1914: April	Sailed for England as member of the Indian National Congress delegation to put their case before the Secretary of State for India, regarding the India Council Reform Bill. Elected chief spokesman and leader of the delegation.
1914: November	Returned to India.
1916: 21 June	Elected to Imperial Legislative Council.
1916: 30–31 December	Presided over Ninth Session of the All-India Muslim League held at Lucknow which approved the 'Lucknow Pact'.
1917: 28 July	Presided over a joint meeting of the All-India Muslim League Council and All-India Congress Committee at Bombay.
1918: 18 April	Miss Ruttenbai, daughter of Sir Dinshaw Petit, a Parsee businessman of Bombay, embraced Islam at Calcutta's Jamia mosque. Maulana Nizam Ahmad Khajandi officiated.
1918: 19 April	Married Miss Ruttenbai at Calcutta.
1918: 11 December	Led demonstration against Lord Willingdon, governor of Bombay.

1919: 28 March	Resigned from Imperial Legislative Council in protest against Rowlatt Act.
1919: 7 June	Came to London as member of a delegation to give evidence before a select committee of the Houses of Parliament on the Montagu Reforms Bill.
1919: 14 August	Birth of Jinnah's daughter, Dina.
1919: 14 November	Returned to India.
1920: 7 September	Left Congress. Presided over the Extraordinary Session of the All-India Muslim League held at Calcutta. Elected permanent President of the All-India Muslim League.
1926: April to August	Remained in England with Ruttie to attend Sandhurst Committee meeting.
1927: 19 January	Sworn in as Member Legislative Assembly, representing Bombay Muslims (urban).
1927: 20 March	Presided over Muslim Conference, Delhi, where Delhi Muslim Proposals were finalized and agreement reached on joint electorate.
1928: January	Separated from his wife, Ruttie.
1928: 5 May	Sailed for London on S. S. Rajputana.
1928: late May	Ruttie Jinnah fell seriosuly ill, admitted to a hospital in Paris.
1928: 12 October	Sailed for India abroad S. S. Zermik.
1928: 26 October	Reached India after his tour of Europe.
1929: 20 February	Death of Mrs Ruttie Jinnah.
1929: 28 March	Presented his famous 'Fourteen Points', regarding Muslim safeguards at League Council Meeting, Delhi.
1930: 7 August	Returned unopposed to India Legislative Council.

1930: 10 September   Nominated as a delegate to the Indian Round
                            Table Conference.

1930: 12 October   Left for London.

1930: 28 October   Arrived in London to attend the Round Table
                            Conference. Was a member of a committee of
                            seven asked to prepare agenda for the conference.
                            Stayed at 3 Whitehall Court, SW 1.

1930: 12 November   Attended the first Round Table Conference,
                            London. Served on three committees: Federal
                            Structure, Defence, and Sindh.

1931: 3 February   Announced intention to stay in London and
                            practice law before the Privy Council.

1931: 21 March   Left for India.

1931: 5 May   Called *ad eundem* by the Inner Temple.

1931: 20 July   Nominated to Federal Structure Committee of
                            the Round Table Conference.

1931: 1 August   Stated that Indian Round Table Conference
                            would fail unless Hindu-Muslim question was
                            settled.

1931: 8 August   UP Muslim Conference at Ahmedabad.

1931: 9 August   Resigned from Legislative Assembly.

1931: 5 September   Left India for England.

1931: 20 September   Arrived in London to join the Federal Structure
                            Committee.

1931: September   Purchased a house in West Heath Road,
                            Hampstead, London.

1931: 16 October   Discussion with Gandhi regarding minorities
                            question.

1931: 30 December   Speech at Indian Students (Indian Engineering
                            Students) Conference, at Torrington Square,
                            London, regarding treatment of labour in British
                            factories.

1933: 6 April	Addressed meeting at Shah Jahan mosque, Woking, London, regarding future of India. Criticized White Paper, etc.
1933: 12 December	Approached by Muslim leaders to return to India where he would be able to restore unity among the Muslim politicians.
1933: 22 December	Left for India.
1934: 4 January	Reached Bombay.
1934: 16 February	Muslim League leaders announced that they were willing to accept him as president of Muslim League.
1934: 24 May	Left for Europe.
1934: 11 October	Elected unopposed (in absentia) Member, Legislative Asembly from Bombay.
1934: 26 December	Returned to Bombay.
1935: 18 February	Speaking at Delhi College, outlined his plea for communal settlement.
1935: April	Tour of the whole country.
1936: 13 April	Severely criticized the new constitution embodied in the Government of India Act of 1935 at the All-India Muslim League. Addressed the Jamiat-ul-Ulema Conference in Delhi explained the 'Policy for Muslims', and criticized the Federal Scheme.
1935: 23 April	Sailed for England on board S. S. Conte Verde.
1935: 24 October	Returned to Bombay on board S. S. Strathnaver.
1936: September	Toured UP and Bengal. Succeeded in reducing differences between various Muslim sects. Presided at a meeting of the Central Parliamentary Board of the All-India Muslim League, Karachi.
1937: January	Announced that Muslims would not be camp-followers of any party or organization.

1937: March	Advised Muslims not to join the Congress strike planned for 1 April.
1937: July	Condemned the Palestine Report.
1937: 24 August	Announced that Muslim representation in Congress ministries unsatisfactory; astonished that no Muslim in Orissa Cabinet.
1937: October	Formally adopted and unfurled the official flag of the All-India Muslim League at special ceremony at Lucknow Session of All-India Muslim League. Jinnah declared that Muslims could expect neither justice nor fair play at the hands of Congress. League changed its creed from full responsible government to full independence.
1937: 30 November	Bitter opposition to federal aspect of new Constitution. Willing to come to agreement with Congress, provided Congress agreed to safeguard minority rights—would co-operate on basis of equality.
1938: February	Possibility of Hindu–Muslim accord as a result of his correspondence with Nehru and Gandhi.
1938: 14 April	Arrived at Calcutta for special session of the Muslim League.
1938: 17 April	In his address to the Muslim League special session, refused to recognize Congress as anything but Hindu body. Would welcome policy of 'Live and Let Live' but Muslims could not accept Congress High Command which had developed into totalitarian and authoritarian organization.
1938: 23 April	Paid tribute to Sir Muhammad Iqbal at a memorial meeting. 'His death an irreparable loss to Muslims in India. He will live as long as Islam will live'.
1938: April–August	Peace talks with Gandhi and Bose.
1938: 6 June	At Muslim League meeting, claimed that Congress represented only Hindus.

1938: 17 June	Correspondence relating to peace talks between him, Gandhi, and Nehru published.
1938: 1 August	Final break with Congress. 'The Congress High Command was puffed up with power, even though it was not yet Hindu Raj, but British Raj—while the intoxication continued, there would be no freedom in India'.
1939: 22 December	In response to Jinnah's call to celebrate the resignation of Congress ministries, Muslims observed Day of Deliverance.
1940: 22–24 March	Presided over Lahore session of All-India Muslim League. Enunciated at this session the concept of Muslim nationhood and demanded the setting up of sovereign Muslim States in majority Muslim areas of subcontinent. The Pakistan resolution was proposed on 23 March and passed at this session on 24 March 1940. 'Geographically contiguous units are demarcated into regions which should be so constituted...the areas in which the Muslims are numerically in a majority, as in the North-Western and Eastern zones of India, should be grouped to constitute independent states in which the Constituent Units shall be autonomous and sovereign'. Given the title of 'Quaid-i-Azam' by the Muslims of India.
1941: 23 March	Celebrated Pakistan Day.
1942: 23 March	Addressed large gathering in Delhi to observe Pakistan Day.
1943: 20 July	An attempt to assassinate Jinnah made by Rafiq Sabir, a Khaksar worker from Lahore, foiled.
1943: 23 September	Declared that recognition of Pakistan scheme was precondition for any settlement in India.
1946: 3 December	Left for London to attend conference between Congress, Akali Dal, and Muslim League.

1946: December	Broke journey at Cairo. Conferred with Egyptian leaders and the Grand Mufti of Palestine, Amin El-Husaini.
1946: 19 December	Returned to Karachi.
1947: 3 June	Partition of India announced by the Viceroy, Lord Mountbatten.
1947: 4 July	Indian Independence Bill passed by the House of Commons.
1947: 14 August	Independence Day of Pakistan. Lord Mountbatten, last Viceroy, transferred power to Constitutional Assembly of Pakistan on behalf of His Majesty's Government. New flag of Pakistan, the crescent and star, hoisted.
1947: 15 August	Jinnah sworn in as the Governor-General of Pakistan.
1948: 1 July	Performed the opening ceremony of the State Bank of Pakistan—the last public function attended by Jinnah.
1948: 14 July	Moved to Ziarat, Balochistan, due to deteriorating health.
1948: 14 August	Message to the nation on its first Independence Day; Jinnah was absent from the celebrations because of his illness.
1948: 11 September	Moved to Karachi from Ziarat.
1948: 11 September	Died in Karachi at 10.25 p.m.
1948: 12 September	Buried with full honours at Karachi.

For dates of Jinnah's education in London, and his travels to and from London, the compiler has relied mainly on original documents, official records, and the index to *The Times*, London

INDEX